Towards Excellence in Early Years Education

This book uniquely describes the work of two Early Years teachers, drawing on their narrative accounts as they robustly describe and analyse their work with young children. Against a backcloth of increasing regulation and inspection of early years care and education, Kathy Goouch emphasises the importance of building authentic relationships with children and their families, explores how play can be promoted as the central site for learning, and shows how professionals can use play to account for children's development and learning.

In analysing the Early Years teachers' narratives, this book explores key themes including:

- Traditional notions of 'teaching' and how they can be redefined
- The significance of talk in children's lives
- Teachers' professional identities
- How children's potential in learning can be achieved through play.

Celebrating knowledge, skills and understanding and re-defining what it means to be a teacher in its broadest sense, this fascinating book brings together research and literature from across disciplines. Containing a foreword by Tricia David, it will be of interest to academics, early years educators and students on early childhood education degree programmes and initial teacher education courses, as well as others concerned with the over-prescriptive nature of early education.

Kathleen Goouch is a Senior Lecturer in Education at Canterbury Christ Church University, UK.

Towards Excellence in Early Years Education

Exploring narratives of experience

Kathleen Goouch

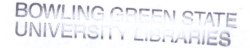
 Routledge
Taylor & Francis Group

LONDON AND NEW YORK

First edition published 2010
by Routledge
2 Park Square, Milton Park, Abingdon, Oxon OX14 4RN

Simultaneously published in the USA and Canada
by Routledge
270 Madison Avenue, New York, NY 10016

Routledge is an imprint of the Taylor & Francis Group, an informa business

© 2010 Kathleen Goouch

Typeset in Garamond by
Taylor & Francis Books
Printed and bound in Great Britain by
TJ International Ltd, Padstow, Cornwall

British Library Cataloguing in Publication Data
A catalogue record for this book is available from the British Library

Library of Congress Cataloging-in-Publication Data
Goouch, Kathy.
   Towards excellence in early years education : exploring narratives of experience / Kathleen Goouch. – 1st ed.
      p. cm.
   Includes bibliographical references.
   1. Early childhood education. I. Title.
   LB1139.23.G662 2010
372.21–dc22   2009053649

ISBN 978-0-415-56607-0 (hbk)
ISBN 978-0-415-56608-7 (pbk)
ISBN 978-0-203-84839-5 (ebk)

For we think back through our mothers if we are women.

All this pitting of sex against sex against sex, of quality against quality; all this claiming of superiority and imputing of inferiority, belong to the private-school stage of human existence where there are 'sides' and it is necessary for one side to beat another side, and of the utmost importance to walk up to a platform and receive from the hands of the Headmaster himself a highly ornamental pot. As people mature they cease to believe in sides or in Headmasters or in highly ornamental pots.

Virginia Woolf
A Room of One's Own, 1929

Contents

Illustrations

Figures

Tables

Box

Foreword

It is a privilege to be invited to write the Foreword for this important, loving account by Kathy Goouch of the work of two remarkable Early Years teachers. The study has a huge contribution to make to our field of Early Childhood Education and Care (ECEC) because it will challenge readers to dig down to their own roots of understanding, their own philosophies, their own underlying values and beliefs about what we do with young children, why – and who we think we are.

Soon after the New Labour Government was elected in 1997, I was invited to a seminar concerned with Primary Education (Early Childhood Education was then largely subsumed under this heading and it is easy to forget how far the field of ECEC has developed since then). However, what I remember most about this seminar was the response of one highly influential leader of industry to my plea that we needed to explore the question 'What is Education *for?*' rather than his taken-for-granted notion that children's schooling exists mainly to prepare them to be workers. He retorted that he had wondered for a moment if he was attending a post-graduate philosophy session.

In the early 1850s, the King of Prussia issued an edict forbidding Friedrich Froebel from training any more young women to work in kindergartens. One can only conclude that the kind of education Froebel was advocating, for the women, the children, or both, constituted some sort of threat – that the King and his overnment feared the consequences of people having the ability to think for themselves and perhaps challenging accepted assumptions.

Both stories highlight the contested nature of Education. Both illustrate the sometimes overt, sometimes covert, power that is used to control access to learning.

This beautiful, meticulous study of the lives and work of two dedicated teachers was conducted in the tradition of respected researchers such as Vi McLean (1991), David Hartley (1993), and the brilliant, late and much-missed Sally Lubeck (1986). You will read how, by sharing conversations, observing Janette and Matthew with the children they taught, asking them to reflect on their actions and their personal histories, Kathy built up a fine-grained narrative of their philosophies, teaching approaches and responses to government requirements. At the same time, Kathy was recording and questioning her own research philosophy and techniques, recognizing deep connections, or parallels, with the two teachers' self-interrogation and with the insights of poets, psychologists and philosophers.

Even if we assume the *Early Years Foundation Stage* (DCSF 2007) was initiated as a well-meaning entitlement for all children, intending the encouragement of play, rather than didactic approaches in ECEC settings, it can be, for many practitioners, constraining and controlling. This is particularly so in resulting misrepresentations of play as something that can be prescribed and planned by adults. While the teachers in this study support and play with the children, multivoicing as they weave their expertise into the children's days, they are at the same time, responsible practitioners capable of noting and recording the children's achievements, relating to parents and co-workers, and above all, learning from the inspiring encounters with very young people which afford us such life-affirming joy.

Tricia David,
Emeritus Professor of Education,
Canterbury Christ Church University, 2010

Preface

I found Jon McGregor's book, *If Nobody Speaks of Remarkable Things* ... (2002), by chance on a supermarket bookshelf. In his book, McGregor used a magnified lens to focus upon a disparate group of people who live in a city street. He captured a sense of their lives as they engage in routines and daily rituals, doing ordinary things. He told how they live alongside each other, occasionally touching each other's lives, occasionally experiencing the colour of another's existence; sometimes speaking. Each detail of each life has been written as an event, a snapshot. The lives of every one of the street's occupants are drawn towards one very important day. McGregor provides such overpowering detail of life in the street that occasional glimpses of dreams and other-worldness seep through too. The book is written in a very poetic prose. The entire text is gripping and extraordinarily beautiful.

This book was inspirational. I had already begun my study of two nursery teachers, both of whom I knew to be interesting. McGregor's work taught me to use a rather bigger lens to look at what many may consider to be ordinary – the detail of encounter. I began to realise that what these 'interesting' teachers were doing was rather extraordinary. It also demonstrated that sometimes by only glancing at the surface of what appears to be a busily teeming existence, it is possible to miss the fundamental core of humanity that exists to support it. While teachers are being scorned for what some may see as the insubstantial surface features of their work, which may be the most simply measurable elements, the exceptional detail of their interactions is sometimes overlooked. McGregor was using one street to be more fully representative of humanity in both its ordinariness and extraordinariness and I suspect that the two teachers that I know are representative of a rather bigger group of exceptional people in their profession. I am unable to know this, only to hope, but my experience has taught me at least to look for extraordinary-ness rather than to only routinely examine the bleakness that is often portrayed.

In this study I have tried to indicate some of the detail of the knowledge and understanding of two brilliant teachers. By the time I had finished listening to them, I knew them to be extraordinary. I hope that this work honours them sufficiently.

The second inspiration for this study came from a very small detail in my own professional life more than twenty years ago. I was a young reception teacher of a very lively group of 4-year-old children. On one particular morning we were busy in the hall, dancing or moving or engaged in some kind of physical activity. I was attached to Emma, a feisty 4-year-old with a clutch of physical disabilities, physically attached as we were busy trying together to travel around the hall, contorting ourselves in whatever was the task for the rest of the class. Obviously, at the same time, I was trying to engage with the other children, encouraging and urging them on. My headteacher, an inspiration for my life and work since, passed through the hall to another classroom but stopped to say in passing 'That's what I call teaching!' I think she was, in part, referring to the inclusiveness of it all but I have since tried to deconstruct her comment, probably because her praise was praise indeed and her judgement was to be trusted. So what was happening in that few minutes that she called 'teaching'? What is 'teaching'?

With the inspiration from these two events, reading McGregor's book and recalling Mrs O'Neil's comment, I have tried to tell my research story and have spoken, in my view, of remarkable people. The practice of early years teachers is increasingly coming under scrutiny as contemporary curriculum designers of this early phase of education introduce the language of market-isation and performativity as the prevailing policy discourse.

This book interrogates the reflexive narratives of two early years profes-sionals. It acknowledges and deconstructs the complexity of the roles played by teachers of young children. The knowledge, skills and the implicit con-cepts and understanding in their practice are identified as they seek to deconstruct their professional lives. The multiple narrative layers at play are disclosed. As well as the often highly influential policy narratives of the time, the project reveals the initial storying narratives on which the reflections are based; descriptions of their practice by two teachers; their reflective ana-lyses; and the researcher's outsider analyses of the picture of practice presented to her.

Together with a consideration of these narrative layers, there is also a range of voices employed by the teachers and evident throughout the study of their practice. The teacher voices are identified as that of narrator of play; voices within play; the creative voice of addressee; their personal voice from lived lives; and the professional voice representing and combining school culture, current policy and that of public servant. This 'polyphony' of voices becomes contingent on the context of the moment and their employment has been described in this study as intuitive. The two teachers demonstrate the breadth and depth of knowledge required to enact multiple roles and to engage in informed, skilful practice. Early career and family mentors were found to be significant in first establishing their professional values. It is, however, the intrinsic rewards of their engagement in play with children which can be seen to nourish the teachers and help the approach to become self-perpetuating.

The key elements identified in this study of the practice of teachers, described here as 'remarkable', are that they engage in all of the following: they help children; they respect children and their families and carers; they respect children's intentions; they engage in narrative constructions; they inhabit risky spaces in order to respond contingently; they are players; and they employ wittingness, both in the classroom and in reflexive opportunities.

These elements, as well as the approach taken to research them, belong to a relational pedagogy which has been used to celebrate a remarkable calibre of early years professional.

Acknowledgements

I am very grateful for the help given to me by my close colleagues who have critically challenged my thinking and encouraged me. I would particularly like to express my gratitude to Tricia David who has inspired and mentored my research and writing for many years and from whom I continue to learn.

I would like to say a very special thank you to my remarkable family, Gill, for her patient and expert technical expertise and guidance, Joe, for our art conversations and Brian, for his unswerving support during times of self-doubt and exhaustion.

I am of course completely indebted to Janette and Matthew; I feel very fortunate to know two such remarkable teachers.

Permissions

I would like to thank the following for granting permission to reproduce material in this work:

Adrian Holliday and Sage Publications for permission to reproduce his diagram 'Positioning the Researcher: Conceptual Framework' from *Doing and Writing Qualitative Research* (2002).

Janet Moyles and Open University Press for kindly giving permission to reproduce her diagram 'Play Theories' from *The Excellence of Play* (2nd edn) (2005).

Every effort has been made to contact copyright holders for their permission to reprint material in this book. The publishers would be grateful to hear from any copyright holder who is not here acknowledged and will undertake to rectify any errors or omissions in future editions of this book.

Introduction

If nobody speaks of remarkable people ...

After all, we learnt all the words we know in the first place only from talking to each other.
(Frayne 2006: 8)

A great deal has been written and published about schools, education, policies and practice and, in particular, the early years field of study in recent years. However, what actually happens to young children in nurseries and reception classes is extremely variable. The now statutory Early Years Foundation Stage (DCSF 2007) remains contentious, representing, as it does, a 'state theory of learning' (Alexander 2010: 307). Such wide-sweeping national policies invariably result in a sometimes very literal translation into practice by conscientious people anxious to be 'correct' in their work. However, if we believe that 'ours is a public system of education which belongs to the people and is not the personal fiefdom of ministers and their unelected advisers' (ibid.: 2), then it is time for those of us with a stake in education – parents and educators – to reconnect with what we understand by education, to reconsider what we would most like our children to experience in relation to education and care, and to re-establish clear criteria for the selection and education of those professionals involved. This last is of special importance at the earliest stages of education where it is believed that 'the quality of the outcomes can be directly tied to the quality of the people working with them' (Owen and Haynes 2010: 206). There is currently enormous pressure on teachers and all those working with children to meet centrally defined and managed targets and yet arguably the single most important target, often overlooked, seems to be to really know and understand the children in their care.

One of the central findings of *Birth to Three Matters: A Review of Literature* (David *et al.* 2003), was that *people* matter to babies and children as they encounter others in their close environments and grow, develop and learn. There is now considerable research evidence which emphasises the social nature of learning (Bruner 1986; Mclean 1991; Dunn 1998, 2004), the importance of attachment to significant adults (David *et al.* 2003; Nutbrown and Page 2008) and the significance of emotional well-being to children's learning potential (Immordino-Yang and Damasio 2007). The work of neuro-science indicates the overwhelming contribution that conversation makes to the growth and shape of children's brain development (Gopnik *et al.* 1999; Greenfield 2000). Observations from everyday family lives are supported by research from across the world which points to the significance of human relationships in children's lives. It seems obvious, then, in attempts to search for qualities in early years education and care, to seek to understand the nature of those people who elect to work with young children, the impetus for that choice and the influences over their practices.

In this book I have attempted to disclose the intentions of the adults in the work they do with young children. From experience of research in education and teaching at different levels it seems that most people find difficulty in articulating their vision, their personal aims, in the work they do every day of their lives. They can often direct you to national directives, school policies or written plans but invariably struggle to voice what they are seeking to achieve in practice. And this is true of people across the professional spectrum. It seems that teachers are unaccustomed to expressing an ideology and instead have become adept at another way of working as they 'simply ventriloquate the new discourse', whatever that might be, which enables them, as Hall claims, to 'masquerade as conforming' (Hall 2007: 97).

My aim in researching the work of professionals working with young children has been to reach beyond the surface of pedagogy and practice in the early years of education and to understand some of the aims, motivations and influences in evidence, through the lenses of two teachers who have shared their stories, their narratives of experience. In this research there was no necessity for masquerade as the research discourse employed had already claimed their excellence. The teachers' job then was simply to deconstruct their work from the inside out, without reference to outcomes of practice or targets, representative of a contemporary discourse of accountability.

It is not my intention to focus too heavily in this work on policy; there are other texts which serve that purpose well (see, for example, Ball 2008; Alexander 2010; Pugh and Duffy 2010). But, before beginning to delve into the research literature and the intricacies of the teachers' narratives, it is important in this chapter to attempt a broad sweep of the view from above, presenting the policy and context in which their work exists, in order to gather a contemporary perspective on the field of early years education and the care of young children in England. These teachers are different, their practice stands out, and their principles of practice are very strongly held and articulated. It is because of this that they need to be viewed against the backdrop of a range of, at times, contrasting but always intense and politically driven national initiatives.

The policy context

Many have written of the inspirational tradition of early years practice in this country and elsewhere, and in particular of the work of Susan Isaacs and the

McMillan sisters, and the enduring influence of Frobel, Montessori and Steiner (see Curtis 1986; Bruce 1987; Nutbrown *et al.* 2008). Indeed, the narratives of their experience and the details of their research still appear as underpinning elements of early childhood studies and in early years teacher education programmes. The research, recorded practice and documentation of such committed professionals, over time and with children, families and communities, while forming part of our educational heritage should perhaps also be a salutary lesson for policy-makers and politicians today. However, for the past 20 years at least, there has been evidence, and concern expressed, at the rather varied nature and quality of provision for the youngest children in society (Curtis 1986; Bennett and Kell 1989; Moyles 1989, 200b; DES 1990; David 1990; Pugh 1992). Physical provision may range, for example, from playgroups held in church halls to independent nursery schools, with geographical location and the economic circumstances of families determining the kind of setting, as well as the amount of time each day a child may spend there (Hurst 1991).

While for some time now there has been political acknowledgement of the importance of the early years of education and care in children's lives, it is sometimes a challenge to see how the effect of this, in terms of central government initiatives and parliamentary Acts, is impacting favourably upon young children and their teachers in their educational settings (David 1990). Table 0.1, while only presenting a sample of some of the most prominent of recent UK government activities, serves to rather starkly illustrate their range and number.

A huge number of initiatives in the field of education and care are in force. Although Table 0.1 only references some of the most significant changes in policy and practice from 1988 to 2008, it does demonstrate how the early years of education, including the training and re-branding of early years professionals, have either been at the forefront of government education policies in recent years or have directly felt the impact of policies relating to school and education. For example, the introduction of the Literacy Strategy in 1998 had an enormous top-down effect on the literacy practices of those working with 3- and 4-year-old children, causing Whitehead to brand it memorably as a 'literacy juggernaut' and to call for 24-hour literacy in nurseries rather than the performance of a literacy hour (Whitehead 1999b: 52). The drawing together of services for children, education, health and care, has been particularly significant, under the recent headline banner of Every Child Matters (Department for Education and Skills 2004). This has initiated work on 'Extended Schools', a central government initiative attempting to bring together community services and agencies working with children of school age, for the apparent benefit of children, families and communities. The policy list also demonstrates the difficulty of working sensitively between definitive prescription, managing equality of provision, progression between stages of care and education and the age of the children in question.

Table 0.1 Policy list

Date, policy/paper/scheme	Description	Comment
1988 Education Reform Act	Introduction of the National Curriculum	Ground-breaking in making a common curriculum statutory – an entitlement for all children – and in establishing the status of core and foundation subjects, subsequently leading to downward pressure to the Early Years.
1989 Children Act	Introduction of Frameworks for Inspection of services for under-8s	Regulation of private and voluntary services, day nurseries, etc.
1990 Starting with Quality	Report on The Education of Children Under Five	Known as The Rumbold Report, it reported on the educational experiences of 3- and 4-year-old children. Highly influential, supported play practices
1992 Education Act	Established the Office for Standards in Education	Ofsted has been one of the highest impacting innovations, regulating with authority the practices of teachers in schools, and later in nurseries and other early years settings
1994 Start Right NNEB – CACHE	Start Right, The Importance of Early Learning, RSA NNEB was disbanded and replaced by CACHE	Recommended a national strategy for improving early childhood education and care
1996 Education Act Desirable Learning Outcomes (DLO)	This Act established the statutory school age as the term following a child's fifth birthday The first national list of outcomes expected of children before statutory school age, SCAA	Other European countries had much later starting ages for formal schooling. Formed the basis for inspection of settings for 4-year-olds
1997 EPPE started Baseline Assessment	Effective Provision of Pre School Education Project, led from Institute of Education, University of London, funded by DfES Accredited scheme of assessment for reception class children	A highly influential, longitudinal study of children in educational settings from 3–11, nationally funded. Range of schemes accredited. Allowed schools to demonstrate 'value added'

Table 0.1 (continued)

Date, policy/paper/scheme	Description	Comment
1998 Free nursery for 4-year-olds (5 x 2½)	650,000 4-year-olds provided with free nursery places for 3 terms before statutory school age.	Many 4-year-old children now in schools.
1998/9 National Literacy and Numeracy Strategies	Literacy and Numeracy Strategies launched, specifying daily literacy and numeracy hours. Schools required to register to opt out of strategies.	The Reception year was included in the Strategies, formalising literacy and numeracy teaching for 4-year-olds and resulting in most classes operating literacy hours with Reception children.
1999 Early Learning Goals	QCA introduced new range of measurable outcomes.	Replaced DLOs, with effect from 2000.
2000 Curriculum Guidance for the Foundation Stage	Established a 'Foundation stage' from 3–end of the reception year. Developed by QCA.	Described 'key learning skills' for young children, 'what might reasonably be expected of children' (Hodge 2000). Introduced the idea of a 'curriculum' for young children, but also guidance'.
2002 Birth to Three	A framework for supporting children in their earliest years.	Introduced materials and research support for those working with children from birth to 3 in a variety of settings.
2003 Excellence + Enjoyment Foundation Stage Profile	Primary Strategy for Schools. QCA introduced new materials.	A new tone to the Strategy work, suggesting creativity and 'enjoyment' could lead to 'excellence'. Introduced 'freedoms' to teachers, in a non-statutory document Common assessment materials distributed to replace 'baseline assessment'.
2004 Every Child Matters EPPE report published	Children's Workforce Development Council (CWDC) set up. New qualification for Children's Centre Leaders	Initiative from central government intended to impact across education, health and care and all services that impact on children's lives. Strong recommendations for high quality nursery care.

Table continued on next page.

Table 0.1 (continued)

Date, policy/paper/scheme	Description	Comment
2005 CWDC National Professional Qualification for Integrated Centre Leadership	Early Years Foundation Stage established National standards described for new professional grades *Independent Review of the Teaching of Reading* (DfES 2006)	Workforce remodelling, part of Every Child Matters initiative. Differentiation beginning in qualifications for those in Early Childhood, Education and Care (ECEC) sector.
2006 Childcare Act Early Years Professional: Rose Review	Statutory Framework introduced and distributed – to be implemented from September 2008	Framework for children from birth to 5, incorporating Birth to Three Framework. Step toward graduate profession. Promoted synthetic phonics as 'first, fast and only' method of teaching reading to young children.
2007–8 EYFS Letters and Sounds		Statutory materials for the first time, establishing content, pedagogy, monitoring and record keeping for all those involved in care and education of children from birth to 5.

Source: Adapted from material in the Early Years Timeline, 1990–2007, Early Childhood Unit, NCB.

Inevitably there has been the potential for conflict between persistent government messages in relation to raising 'standards' in subjects, particularly literacy and numeracy, measured by Standard Attainment Tests (QCA 2008), and the strong lobby from the early years community of research and practice (see, for example, the Open EYE campaign 2007) who promote an approach that would be similar to a 'social pedagogic' approach found in other European countries. In this social pedagogic approach, the 'quality of life in the setting, children's well being and social development and a play-based flexible pedagogy' (David and Powell 2005) are the national emphases. In her introduction to the Curriculum Guidance for the Foundation Stage in 2000, the then Under-Secretary of State for Employment and Equal Opportunities, Margaret Hodge, talks of the Foundation Stage as a time for developing 'skills', particularly 'early communication, literacy and numeracy skills that will prepare young children for Key Stage 1 of the National Curriculum' (Hodge, 2000). These ideas about readiness and steps towards a curriculum are rather distant from, for example, the introduction to the Swedish early years curriculum which has a different emphasis:

> Democracy forms the foundation of the preschool. For this reason, all preschool activity should be carried out in accordance with fundamental democratic values. Each and everyone working in the preschool should promote respect for the intrinsic value of each person, as well as respect for our shared environment
>
> An important task of the preschool is to establish and help children acquire the values on which our society is based. The inviolability of human life, individual freedom and integrity, the equal value of all people, equality between the genders as well as solidarity with the weak and vulnerable are all values that the preschool should actively promote in its work with children.
>
> (OECD 2006: 219)

Values are central to this introductory section of the Swedish curriculum document and they are identified clearly as underpinning Swedish society and therefore important for young children to grasp at the earliest stage, during pre-school. In his report for the Organisation for Economic Co-operation and Development, Bennett makes a strong distinction between those countries who engage in the 'schoolification' (Bennett and OECD 2006: 62) of early childhood education and care and those who operate in the 'Nordic tradition'. Bennett's descriptions are particularly relevant as he analyses elements from each tradition, including how children and childhood are constructed. In his chapter 'Features of two curricular traditions', the 'readiness for school tradition' describes understandings of the child and childhood in this way:

> The child as a young person to be formed, as an investment in the future of society; the productive knowledge worker, the compliant well-behaved citizen ... A benevolent, utilitarian approach to childhood in which State and adult purposes are fore grounded. Pedagogy focused on 'useful' learning, readiness for school, a tendency to privilege indoors learning.
>
> (ibid.: 141)

In contrast to this, 'The Nordic tradition' is seen to construct children differently:

> The child as a subject of rights: autonomy, well being ... the right to growth on the child's own premises. The child as agent of his/her own learning, a rich child with natural learning and research strategies ... The child as member of a caring community of peers and adults, in which the influence of the child is sought. An outdoors child of pleasure and freedom. A time for childhood that can never be repeated.
>
> (ibid.: 141)

The former describes a utilitarian approach with a lack of interest evident there in childhood as a time to be recognised and enjoyed in itself, but instead represents childhood as a short, directed passage towards compliance and citizenship. This is very different from the Nordic tradition described above where the child appears to have rights and agency and the stage of childhood is acknowledged as important. The five key outcomes of Every Child Matters – be healthy, stay safe, enjoy and achieve, make a positive contribution and achieve economic well-being (DfES 2004) – also provide evidence of where the main concerns are of the government, in England, at this moment in history. Clear national aims for the care and education of young children, however, are hard to determine. While, as demonstrated above, policy follows routinely on policy and political rhetoric on the subject is often heard, it is difficult to determine whether the fundamental aim is to provide child care in order to support the employment of women; provide child care and education in order to change or at least influence the lives of children; provide child care and education to work towards the eradication of child poverty; or the provision of an education service to secure an early start to formal learning (see Duffy 2010). It could be argued that all of these are important aims and should all be promoted equally, although some may result in conflicting outcomes for children. However, it is also important to be clear about the overarching aims of society as well as contemporary national objectives in order that what counts as 'quality' in early years education and care provision can be properly understood. In addition, if what is intended for children is clear, then a workforce, or better still – a profession – to support those intentions can be effectively prepared and supported. It may be, however, that the muddle surrounding national aims is effective in keeping some of these key challenges at bay:

1 Sustainability and affordability.
2 Recruitment, training and remunerating a workforce.
3 Mapping the range of early years services with schools.
4 Meeting the needs of both parents and children.

(Adapted from Pugh 2010)

While considerable effort has been made to increase the qualifications of those working with young children, serious financial investment remains a huge stumbling block to ensuring that professionals are well educated, employed, rewarded and supported effectively to work with the youngest children. Of the legislation, there has been considerable concern expressed in recent research relating to 'professionalism' and the ways in which education and the teaching profession are becoming 'marketised' (Whittey 1997) and this of course resonates in the early years field where 'provision' has become synonymous in some cases with 'business', and carries with it all the implications of affordability in relation to staffing. Recruiting, retaining and supporting the professional development of staff, particularly in the private, voluntary and independent sector of provision, continue to present challenges. Particularly significant has been the new work on the professional status of those in this sector and the attempt to create a graduate profession, or at least at this stage a graduate-led profession, for work with the youngest, and potentially most vulnerable, children in society. Arguably, this phase would require the most qualified and the highest quality of professional. Combined with this is the work of the Children's Workforce Development Council (CWDC) which claims:

> to improve the lives of children, young people, their families and carers by ensuring that all people working with them have the best possible training, qualifications, support and advice. It also helps children and young people's organisations and services to work together better so that the child is at the centre of all services.
>
> (Children's Workforce Development Council 2008)

This kind of state-led altruism is interesting if questionable. It may depend on what 'the best possible training' is seen to be and who is offering support and advice. For example, Gibson and Patrick's discussion of a 'scripted pedagogy' claims that 'remodelling may signify the structured withering of reflection upon pedagogical discourses and the deferment to national directives' (2008: 26). Questions also need to be raised in relation to the authoring of such scripts and levels of support for those professionals whose job it is to interpret them to the best of their abilities and to the benefit of young children. Implicit also in this discussion are hard questions about the values and intentions underpinning the production of a scripted pedagogy and whose interests are served by the potential of a 'structured withering of reflection'.

Understanding 'good' practice and remarkable people

In the midst of the tensions between the enormous range of public policy and practice, I knew of at least two nursery teachers who were engaging in a particular kind of pedagogy. This study, in broad terms, is an attempt to understand teaching and teachers in the early years of education and to help in redefining these complex terms for people working in this phase. It sets out to achieve this through examining the two teachers' reflective narratives of their experiences as teachers of nursery-aged children in England. They have been asked individually and collaboratively to engage in reconstructing and accounting for their practice through the expression and analysis of their own developing philosophy of the aims of education. Essentially they respond to the question of how young children develop and learn and their own roles in this. Exploring issues of identity, from the inside out and the outside in, is central to the work, that is, inviting the teachers to talk about themselves and who they think they are within the framework of research and literature that explores the nature of teaching, teachers and professionalism and under-scores the nature of the work expected of teachers of young children, their roles and responsibilities. The teachers' identities are thus examined through their own presentation of their own stories, their professional narratives.

I have attempted to determine, through reflective research conversations, the nature of their practice, their 'context of influence' (Bryan 2004), the knowledge and skills that they apply in their practice and their own levels of 'wittingness' (Peters 1966: 42), that is, their own understanding of what they are doing and why they are working in a particular way. The wittingness demonstrated in these teachers' work has come to represent a highly significant professional attribute.

The 'quest' in this study has been to critically examine existing literature relating to early years education and professionalism as well as the narratives of teaching and learning in the practice and in the professional reflections of the two early years teachers in the hope of understanding their intentions, the influences on them in terms of policies, research evidence, training, mentors and life experiences. The two key questions I asked them in relation to their professional practice are: 'Who do you think you are?' and 'What do you believe you are doing?' The process of gathering the answers to these two questions and closely analysing the responses while placing this research within the framework of early years research and policy is the essence of this book.

The methods employed to harness the teachers' stories and the methodo-logical stance taken are detailed in the Appendix for those readers interested in an account of the process of study. In brief, the teachers were asked to video their own practice, they were observed playing with children, they were interviewed individually and engaged in joint research conversations. The teachers were not randomly selected. They were specifically chosen because they were known to be good teachers – through reputation, through Ofsted reports, reports from their managers, through promotion and through personal knowledge. Why they were considered to be good was the subject of research. In this book, I have used the terms 'teachers' and 'teaching' very broadly to encompass all professionals working with children in institutional settings and in order to distinguish the two people on which my research is based I refer to them frequently as 'my teachers'. It is notoriously difficult to find a noun to encompass all those who work with and educate children and I have met those who object to being described as a teacher, as they argue that their work does not involve what they understand by the term 'teaching', which often equates in people's minds with 'instruction' or didactic methods. I hope that the celebration of the work of the two teachers here reassures them and justifies my insistence on the term.

Structure of the book

The book is divided into two parts. In Part I, the background and field of study are considered. In Chapter 1, the ideological position that I have taken in relation to my knowledge of the field of study is made clear and the nature of the pedagogical framework within which this book has been constructed is detailed. Chapter 1 describes the context of references from which the study has grown, clearly laying bare the bias that would inevitably be evident in any research. An example of multiple layers of narrative, a term used elsewhere in this work, is given.

The early years field of research and study has grown enormously in the past 20 years or so and much of this has been reported and published. While it may be difficult for those engaged in educational research to proffer opinion or judgement on other fields of scientific enquiry, everybody is an expert in education! Everybody has been to school; many are parents of children who have been to school or are of school age and this seems to qualify a range of professionals, and others, to feel empowered in their views. Philosophers, sociologists and psychologists often feel particularly equipped to determine appropriate teaching practice (see, for example, the concluding comments in Ellis 2007: 295). Examples from these fields of research need to be considered alongside the work of experts in the early years research field itself, of which there are many. There are also seminal works that need to be considered and weighed anew in relation to contemporary studies, in work based on, for example, the advancement of technology and science as well as the breadth of research and enquiry now being undertaken to understand brain growth and activity in babies, and the cultural learning of young children.

In Chapters 2, 3 and 4 this broad field of research and enquiry is identified and explored, with three clear areas defined for examination and discussion: (1) Stories, Storying and Storytellers; (2) Playful Pedagogies; and, finally, (3) Talk.

At the end of Part I, Chapter 5 relates to the nature of the research process itself. In this chapter the idea of a relational research enquiry is introduced which was designed to mirror the relational pedagogy that was encountered in practice. While it may be implicitly acknowledged that all authors of educational texts have a position or stance from which they research and report, in this chapter that stance is made explicit in order to be completely clear that researcher/author identity has a role to play in every educational tract or text. The intention is not to patronise readers but simply to reflect honestly on the writing of such a research report. Chapter 5 then details this reflective process and attempts to set the research data itself into this context.

Part II turns attention from the theory and government policies to the actual hands-on, daily experience of teaching in action employed by the two teachers studied, Janette and Matthew. Chapter 6 offers empirical data from the research project, analysis of these teachers' practices, and a discussion of key threads and themes. Chapter 7 discusses the introspection of Janette and Matthew as they reflect on their practice. Finally, in Chapter 8, conclusions are drawn from the study and some comments are made about the implications at broad, local and individual levels of engagement. The intention overall in this book is to draw down the discussion from the broadest policy and research literature relating to pedagogy and practice to the finest point, that is to the point of engagement between adult(s) and child(ren) and to identify the understanding, the intentions and the narratives of influence that support it. And, of course, also to celebrate the two remarkable teachers who engaged in the research process. The Appendix details the methodology used in this project as an aid to other researchers.

Summary

This introduction has offered a context for the study of the narratives of experience of two teaching professionals working with young children in nursery settings and has done the following:

1   presented a broad policy framework within which this study is situated;
2   briefly considered the impact of recent, generic education and social care policies on early years education in England;
3   offered the contrasting traditions of Nordic policy documentation with that of England, with reference to the OECD Report (Bennett and OECD 2006);
4   introduced the subject of study, that is, the focus on two early years teachers and their professional narratives.

Research and the early learning landscape

Chapter 1

Reflections on the pedagogical context

An organic landscape?

This chapter provides the foundations on which the rest of the book is based and introduces many of the ideas and terms of reference further examined in the rest of Part I and illustrated from practice in Part II.

Through my own experience as a teacher, my experience with student teachers and with practising teachers, I have come to believe that teachers are not all of one 'tribe', who share rituals, customs, discourse and traditions. Instead, there are individuals, people, professionals who select, shape, reshape and transcend ways of working so that any sense of 'tribal morality' is 'peripheral to [their] personal integrity' (Allport 1955: 34). I have also begun to understand Bruner's claim that 'selfhood is profoundly relational' and that the 'construction of selfhood cannot proceed without a capacity to narrate' (Bruner 2002: 86). This must be particularly true of teachers and others working within a professional community of practice (Wenger 1998), whose narrations inevitably find a level of interface from which individual narratives rebound and reform. This idea of self-making through narrative, in my study, can be generally applied to the children, their teachers and their researcher, which is itself the subject of analysis.

Where are we now?

In recent years there has been a closer scrutiny of teachers and teaching than I have previously witnessed in more than 30 years of work in the field of education. As a consequence of this and the proliferation of policy initiatives illustrated earlier, there appears to be more compliance by teachers with national programmes and government initiatives. However, in the early years of education there appears still to be an opportunity, however small and potentially short-lived, to account for children's learning through a pedagogy steeped in play and led by children, and to create classroom cultures that allow children to spend time learning before they encounter classrooms boundaried by a culture of performance, driven by testing and results. Paradoxically, it is also possible in many early years school and nursery settings to witness how teachers claim the play discourse, and the play spaces – leading, directing, redirecting, approving or rejecting children's utterances and activities as they attempt to identify and work, in a Vygotskian sense, within children's 'zone of proximal development'. This may take children's performances towards pre-ordained curricula outcomes, and 'allowing' play, while accounting for it in nationally recognised terms, enables teachers to be creatively compliant. However, this approach also appropriates or hijacks children's play intentions and sends direct messages in relation to choice, freedom, control and dominance. The influences on teachers to engage in this kind of practice are discussed in the following chapters. In such circumstances, Wertsch asks the 'Bakhtinian' question 'Who is doing the talking?' and challenges the privileging of some texts and some speech genres over others (Wertsch 1991). These ideas will also be explored more fully in subsequent chapters but questions of voice and power are embedded throughout.

In spite of, or perhaps because of, very tight control of curriculum detail, pedagogy and policy, there remain individual teachers who respectfully join with children in play, engage in intimate conversations and are themselves responsive to children's directions, language and intentions without appropriating the play for their own purposes. Such teachers, who engage in serious and complex play interactions and narrative co-constructions with young children, are rare but are still to be found in some early years settings. This kind of organic pedagogy, developing out of the moment, may be described as 'intuitive' (Atkinson and Claxton 2000) or, indeed, intuition may only be part of the pedagogic story, with other influences and other imperatives yet to be described. The two teachers who have agreed to participate in this research, Janette and Matthew, have not been chosen randomly, but have instead been identified as intuitive teachers who engage in such an organic pedagogy and who involve themselves in serious and complex play interactions and narrative co-constructions with young children.

There appear to be some key characteristics of the context and practice created by *intuitive* teachers. These include wide-ranging play areas generously resourced with story props (for example, traditional 'home corner' accessories, dolls and teddies), blocks and boxes, blankets and cushions, physical space and, most significantly, dedicated adult time – for incidental as well as focused interactions. Another common characteristic is the respectful nature of the interactive events, with teachers attentively listening, being themselves directed, cooperating and also at times offering guidance and possible solutions. It seems as if the teachers are servicing the learning and the learners. The nature of such service is worthy of very close scrutiny if it is not to be mistaken for a *laissez-faire* approach to teaching and learning and it is this that I intend to examine in the research conversations and observations that follow in Part II.

Policy and play

In the *Early Years Foundation Stage Framework* (Department for Children, Schools and Families 2007), while there is clearly evidence of influence from central government in the form of the *Independent Review of the Teaching of Early Reading* (Department for Education and Skills 2006), there remains a robust commitment to some sound principles of early education, particularly in relation to the connectedness of children's development and learning, the acknowledgement that children learn at their own pace, the importance of enabling children to develop a positive sense of self and the central idea that learning most often occurs in social contexts. There are still, however, conflicting views being represented and the discourse in relation to play remains a challenge to some of us working and researching in the field. In this policy document (Department for Children, Schools and Families 2007) there are repeated references to 'planned, purposeful play' (ibid.: 11, 2.5) and the *Independent Review of Early Reading* refers to 'instructive learning play environments' (Department for Education and Skills 2006: 105). This contradictory use of terminology, the conflation of 'instructive' and 'planned' with play, appears to emanate from the difficulties that we have in deciding what we (that is, society, represented by a democratically elected government and their civil servants) want from and for children, childhood and schooling. The recent, much heralded and frequently cited, DfES-funded Effective Provision of Pre-School Education study (EPPE, Sylva *et al.* 2004) and Researching Effective Pedagogy in the Early Years (REPEY, Siraj-Blatchford *et al.* 2004) concluded first that 'good quality provision' can help to limit the effects of social disadvantage and then, most significantly:

> The provision of exploratory play environments (e.g. sand/water play) will only be 'effective' if the materials/ apparatus are chosen carefully to provide cognitive challenge within the zone of proximal development *and* positive outcomes for the activity are either modelled, demonstrated, explained or otherwise identified in the children's experiences and actions, and encouraged.
>
> (Siraj-Blatchford and Sylva 2004: 727)

Although this statement is then qualified slightly, it remains the case that such predetermined outcomes, the intentions of teachers following a curriculum, extolling behaviours and language that are preconceived to be 'appropriate', are all intended to precede or potentially overpower the intentionality of the child. It seems that teachers are caught in a dichotomy of either planning to allow play in unregulated, and therefore by association, unimportant corners of the classroom and the curriculum classroom (an example of this may be 'golden time') or allowing play as long as it fulfils, or can be shaped towards, preordained curricula intentions – the 'positive outcomes' to be encouraged, above. However, in some definitions, play is defined as being 'self-chosen; risk-free; totally engrossing; interesting and meaningful to the learner; intellectually demanding; set in a community of other 'players' with a shared understanding; more transparent to the player than to the adults' (Smidt

2003: 121) which would not fit neatly into either of the above so-called play pedagogies.

Currently, there also seems to be an 'inter-discipline' battle between psychologists, some of whom claim that, for example, the teaching of reading is straightforward if teachers simply deliver the code to children at the earliest possible opportunity and certainly before the age of 5, as recommended by the *Independent Review of Early Reading* (Department for Education and Skills 2006), and educators and educationalists who claim that *how* this occurs is as important as how early it occurs. It is interesting to see, in this new age of fascinating insights from neuro-science and increasing technological support for understanding how we develop, think and learn, that there remains a naïve view that 'instruction' is synonymous with 'teaching' and that children therefore learn when 'taught', in a straightforward causal way. As Hall reminds us, 'Teaching is not an explanation for learning. Teaching is neither necessary nor sufficient for learning to occur' (2007: 94).

Understanding and conceptualising pedagogy have never been more important or more widely challenged than now. In his examination of international pedagogy, Alexander defines six pedagogical values which he claims 'reflect views on the purposes of education, the nature of knowledge and the relationship of teachers and learner' (2003: 26):

- *Teaching as transmission* sees education primarily as a process of instructing children to absorb, replicate and apply basic information and skills.
- *Teaching as induction* sees education as the means of providing access to, and passing on from one generation to the next, the culture's stock of high status knowledge, for example, in literature, the arts, humanities and the sciences.
- *Teaching as democracy* in action reflects the Deweyan idea that teachers and students jointly create knowledge and understanding rather than relating to one another as authoritative source of knowledge and its passive recipient.
- *Teaching as developmental facilitation* guides the teacher by principles which are psychological (and more specifically Piagetian) rather than social or epistemological. The teacher respects and nurtures individual differences and waits until children are ready to move on rather than pressing them to do so.
- *Teaching as acceleration*, in contrast, implements the Vygotskian principle that education is planned and guided acculturation rather than facilitated 'natural' development, and indeed that the teacher seeks to outpace development rather than follow it.
- *Teaching as technique*, finally, is relatively neutral in its stance on society, knowledge and the child. Here the important issue is the efficiency of teaching regardless of the content of values, and to that end matters such as structure, the economic use of time and space, carefully graduated tasks, regular assessment and clear feedback are more pressing than ideas such as democracy, autonomy, development or the disciplines.

(ibid.: 26)

Alexander seeks to compare pedagogy in England, France and Russia and draws on the values listed above to frame this comparative study. However, this list is only useful in the context of this study as it defines characteristics of teaching found in practice and can be used, not to pass judgement on teachers or to identify a 'correct' approach, but instead to support the identification of aspects of practice in order to understand where practice may be located in order to develop an ideological stance, which, it could be argued, is missing from some teachers' work. And in play the world of teaching and learning becomes a much more complex site. In play, power changes hands, from adult to child, and 'in classes where the how is more important than the what, the journey more valuable than the destination, good educators value what it is that children choose to do and then seek to understand and extend it' (Smidt 2003: 125). Values and aims then become significantly more difficult to characterise simply within discretely identified definitions, as above, although a pedagogy that allows play may be closer to Dewey's theories than any other.

Such narrow views and systems of accountability for practice in evidence exist that simple causal connections appear attractive, that is, teachers teach and so learners learn; with the implication that if children are unable to achieve specified objectives in this way and at the time also specified, that they, or indeed their teachers, are in some way deficient. However, as Hall explains in her discussion of literacy policy, 'the notion of "doing" rather than "knowing" gets to the point of it' (Hall 2007: 94), that is 'doing phonics as opposed to having acquired phonic knowledge' (ibid.: 94). And equally this notion could be applied to the fact that some teachers 'do' what is required of them, literally, and others seek to participate in the knowledge debate, what is to be known and how that may occur, described by Sachs as 'activist teachers' (Sachs 2003).

Broader references

The approach that I have described above as 'organic' and 'intuitive' is particularly worthy of study, first, because I am making claims for it to be of enormous value to children but also, second, because it is happening in a particular climate – of political certainties in relation to education, of robust managerial drives towards prescriptive curricula and tightly controlled levels of accountability. All of this seems to be counter to intuitive practices and organic pedagogy. The dominant culture, and therefore the dominant discourse, in contemporary educational policy recognise only technicist/rationalist ideologies. Further, it is clear that in some educational fields, for example primary literacy education, where central government has taken new and overarching control, 'teachers may be regarded as blank slates, or "palimpsests", tablets on which successive scripts are written' (Bryan 2004: 143). In this study, I intend to discover whether my two teachers have escaped such government inscription and, if they have, is it because they are working with the youngest children or because of who they are, as people and as teachers?

In conversation, the teachers talk about satisfying children's interests but they also express the ways that this fits into a bigger picture, that is they feel themselves to be considering 'the interests of children, what is in their interest and what is in the public interest' (Peters 1966: 167). In order to fulfil the enormity and the multi-faceted nature of this claim, they are making judgements, mostly unconsciously it seems, about values and beliefs they wish to impart and support in their practice with young children. They are accomplishing all of this, however, by occupying *'the plane of the personal'* rather than a 'purely functional position' (ibid.: 94) and that, perhaps, marks them as different from other teaching professionals. The 'plane of the personal' in these early years contexts is evident at all levels, in all interactions spoken and otherwise, but takes a very visible form in activities that involve storying, story play or play narratives, consciously valued and given time and both physical and conceptual space by the teachers being studied. It is during these moments of often incidental intimacy between the teacher and one child or an infinite number of children, when the children's own discourse takes precedence, their intentions are paramount and their choices apparent, that an attendant aspect of the teachers' role becomes visible. And it is these storying moments that I have focused my attention on and the principles upon which such pedagogy is based.

Narratives

Any research study of teaching and learning must inevitably contain very complex layers of narrative, often at least three and potentially as many as eight narrative layers. These are non-hierarchical and could be the narratives of: (1) the children; (2) their teachers; (3) the researcher; (4) parents/family; (5) the school/institution; (6) local policy; (7) national policy; and (8) international policy. It might be tempting to include the narrative voices of all of the research giants, upon whose intellectual searches the study would also rest – though this might reach very large numbers. It might instead be safer to say that the author's voice attempts to faithfully reflect these voices. The first three layers, however, are non-negotiable.

One interesting example of multiple narratives, developed over a very small aspect of practice, may be this case study. A teacher moved from a predominantly white middle-class country town school to an urban multi-ethnic district. He had been used to the children addressing him by his first name. When he tried to introduce this into his new school practice, the children insisted on prefacing his name with 'Mr', calling him 'Mr Matthew'. In this example, the children constructed the initial narrative, i.e. the creation of his new name and the teacher told the story, reflecting the importance in which he held it. Finally, the researcher documented it, knowing it to be of significance for several reasons: because it represents the teacher's interest in creating close interpersonal and non-'teacherly' relations with the children; because it signified the different ways in which children view teachers in different neighbourhoods; because it challenged the teacher in relation to how he had viewed children and assumptions he had made, because it very clearly represented how children create their own reality, piecing together information from different sources; because it made Matthew and I smile together at children's precocious persistence. Arguably, these reasons all rest on other wide-ranging research findings, across disciplines, including socio-cultural (the positioning of teaching professionals in society), psychological (what it means to individuals and their sense of identity in their relationships) and philosophical (how we conceive of educational theory).

In theory, it would be interesting to consult the parents and families of the children to gauge their opinions of how they believe their children should address their teacher. It would also be appropriate to look at policy narratives – locally, nationally and internationally – in order to gather information about guidance or prescription to teachers in relation to this issue. The layered nature of influences on the classroom narrative then becomes acutely visible, although there would be still more to reveal. The cultural influences on families and children, teachers and researchers in relation to power and authority, the social expectations, and issues of class and culture would all need to be explored in order to fully understand why the children elected to use this form of address to their teacher and why this became interesting to document. Finally, it also signifies how a small piece of dialogic evidence opens up for examination the affective nature of teaching and learning.

Following the trail described above is not the prime interest here, although the fact that there exists such a trail *is* interesting. The reported fact, that the teacher requested to be addressed by his name and the children's response to that, is enough in this instance to provide just another piece of the puzzle that represents the whole picture – of who the teachers are who attempt to behave in this 'relational' way with young children. Who are the teachers who occupy the 'plane of the personal' in their classrooms and why do they do so?

The argument for affective educational practices and the use of story

It is easy to see how children, defining their own space, time and narrative, will inevitably be affectively involved in their play practice. By being close to, listening to, playing with and responding to children, it seems that it must be impossible for teachers to be disengaged from them. But 'engagement' may imply merely 'surveillance' in Bernstein's terms (1997: 60), or merely allowing such events to occur. Affective engagement requires rather more. It demands empathy and emotional connection with children as players; genuine interest in their play; attention to their problems and their solutions;

and acute sensitivity. This level of professional activity also requires professional 'know how', that is, knowledge of children and childhood, of development and learning, of skills and their application, together with pedagogical understandings.

Attention to emotion rather than, or in addition to, technical or rational acts and involvement can sometimes be considered of little or lesser importance in educational practice. However, some research is now providing new information making closer connections between cognitive development and emotion. While teachers may intuitively feel that affect is important in their work with children, the following rather interesting analogy has been made to claim an absolutely fundamental role for emotion in education:

> Emotions are not just messy toddlers in a china shop, running around breaking and obscuring delicate cognitive glassware. Instead, they are more like the shelves underlying the glassware; without them cognition lacks support.
>
> (Immordino-Yang and Damasio 2007: 5)

In their recent research from neuro-science, Immordino-Yang and Damasio have worked with brain-damaged adults and children. The results of their studies pointed to the fact that emotion is essential in cognitive development, decision-making, problem-solving, social interactions and social functioning. This research with 'damaged' patients illuminates 'the nested relationship' between emotion and cognition. Indeed, the findings from their study confirm that 'neither learning nor recall happen in a purely rational domain, divorced from emotion' and that if educators attempt to create a purely 'rational domain', then they will be encouraging children to 'develop the sorts of knowledge that inherently do not transfer well to real world situations'. Further, they argue that 'knowledge and reasoning divorced from emotional implications and learning lack meaning and motivation and are of little use in the real world (ibid.: 9). These are grave warnings for teachers and their managers and clearly indicate the need for closely contextualised and effective teaching and learning events.

Teachers

The argument, to combine the rational with the emotional, would equally apply to the education of teachers. Education is too important to leave in the hands of just anyone, but what then are the teacher traits that are most useful in education, specifically in early years education? To understand this it is important to try to understand the aims of education, as successive governments have defined them, and the purposes of schools in contemporary society. Are they merely instrumental, as Peters claimed, acting as 'orphanages for children with parents' (Peters 1966: 167), do they simply need to 'have regard to the needs of the community for citizens who are trained in specific ways' (ibid.: 167) or is education part of the function of schools, as one may assume? Peters' philosophical discussion of the nature of education likens initiation to education:

> Just as 'education' requires that those who are educated should be brought to this state by various processes which only have in common the minimum requirements of wittingness and voluntariness, so too does 'initiation' convey the same suggestion of being placed on the inside of a form of thought or awareness by a wide variety of processes which at least involve some kind of consciousness and consent on the part of the initiate.
>
> (ibid.: 54)

While this still suggests actions being acted out on the child (or the initiate), who would be 'brought to this state', notions of 'wittingness' and 'voluntariness' and being taken 'inside of a form of thought' are distinctly more indicative of a shared journey than a didactic delivery of a crudely defined body of knowledge. Indeed, Peters' term 'wittingness' is harnessed later in my study as being distinctly worthy of close interrogation. It is a short step then to the idea that a 'good teacher is a guide who helps others to dispense with his services' (ibid.: 53), although the suggestion that an element of a teacher's role would be that of guide is neither new nor universally accepted in current political terms. Equally, the idea that 'teachers can no longer be trained, they have to be educated' (ibid.: 92) would be anathema to many politicians and contemporary policy-makers who have persistently sought to bury such ideas.

In my study, the teachers claim to have drawn their practice from their own values and beliefs about how best children can be helped to think and learn. Through the consistent nourishment of trusting relationships they are drawn into play and alongside players, they are consulted by children, often conscripted, confided in and sometimes dismissed. While it may be uplifting in some sense to consider that 'the essential feature of education ... consists in experienced persons *turning the eye of others outwards*' (ibid.: 54, my italics), it may be more realistic in the focus on narrative co-constructions to see teacher-player and child-player as conspirators striving together for an acceptable, constructed meaning. For the teachers in this study, this achievement is only part, although an important part, of their professional role. As the teachers later claim, they are also striving to be 'alert to likelihoods', 'best guessing their [children's] intentions', 'observing, listening and making sense' of what they see, making sure that children's 'basic needs are met', 'reflecting, thinking, knowing why they're doing what they're doing', and much more. These highly skilled professionals, whether performing as 'addressees' or 'narrators', have as the core of their role to serve children in all matters and manners of learning.

As previously stated, the aims of education in this country are still at best unclear. The politics of education, the instrumental use of schooling as 'orphanages for children with parents' (ibid.: 167), to serve the economic needs of society, is a fundamentally challenging concept. Currently schools are being used to transmit a body of knowledge that is particularly valued now, in England. This is evidenced by the current narrow emphases on literacy (the focus remaining on the teaching of reading) and numeracy (the focus here on knowledge of numbers). The functional nature of the curriculum, the tested aspects of curriculum and rationalisation of content and pedagogy (the Rose Review, DfES 2006, would be an example of this) have created a new role for new education professionals. All of those working in schools and early years settings today do not need to have qualified teacher status and there is an even more substantial move towards a functional view of schooling than in previous recent history (Gibson and Patrick 2008).

Combined with these political ambitions for education there appears to be an almost moral panic in society generally that children are escaping control and that their behaviour needs to be modified (see, for example, BBC 2008) and that children and their families are not adhering to cultural expectations (see, for example, BBC 2003). While it is also widely asserted that children need to play, justifying play in educational institutions (for example, nurseries and reception classes) remains a problem. The contested place of play in an education system seems to be accompanied by muddled aims, which results in a confused early years curriculum, whose language purports to serve the needs of children, to centralise play, yet wraps it in tight structures. Such a curriculum is in danger of missing out the intentionality of children's activities and the volitional nature of learning.

Very strong policy imperatives have been emanating from central government to effect change in early years education in England. The political rhetoric of the moment seems to be offering teachers of young children conflicting messages, sometimes misappropriating the discourse of the research field but generally urging forward a standards agenda, irrespective of children's circumstances, their family or cultural context, their economic background or their early experiences. In his maiden speech, the Secretary of State for Children, Schools and Families, Ed Balls, claimed his new department *is* the *Every Child Matters* Department and described the choice between taking account of 'standards' and taking into account the 'whole view of the child' as futile and 'old-fashioned'. He declared the need to 'break down the false divide between policies to support achievement and policies to support well-being' (Balls 2007). However, in a powerful critique of the 'instrumentalisation of the expressive' Hartley (2006: 61) presents an argument to demonstrate how the creative or expressive arts are now being commodified to satisfy corporate, commercial and other newly perceived 'performative purposes'. Affective education then becomes of worth only if it satisfies the needs of the economic state and the 'knowledge economy'. Hartley concludes that 'creativity and emotional literacy are being "attached" to an educational practice which remains decidedly performance-driven, standardized and monitored' (ibid.: 69). Within this argument, political rhetoric – and the current Secretary of State's apparently new concerns with a holistic view of education – take on new meaning.

In reality, however, the only systems of accountability currently being addressed in schools in England are controlled very carefully by the Office for Standards in Education (OfSTED, which also monitors nursery provision), the Training and Development Agency and the publication of league tables. At every level 'the discourse of current and recent reforms couches all initiatives in terms of human capital and ensures that only government voices are heard' (Hall 2004: 1), thus diminishing or rendering invalid or weak any attempt to value children's achievements and their teachers' performances in alternate ways. Teachers who only attend to the discourse of 'official science' (Wertsch 1991: 137) and become 'restricted professionals' (Hall 2004: 48) are in danger of also becoming highly successful in identifying zones into which government agencies require children to move and develop.

The political arguments, simplifying complex teaching processes into reductionist 'common-sense' terms, equating teaching with instruction and mocking early years practitioners as not being involved in 'rocket science' (Department for Education and Skills 2006) need to be balanced by carefully constructed research to inform and support teachers of young children who are struggling to defend and account for their practice against a growing political storm. The post-structuralist ideas of Foucault expose 'seemingly "natural" or "logical" forms of knowledge' as the language of social control (Hughes and Sharrock 1997: 188) or 'dominant discursive regimes' (Dahlberg et al. 1999: 139). If 'language is ideology' (Hughes and Sharrock 1997: 180), then

> knowledge, or what is defined as legitimate knowledge ... not only shapes our understanding of the world by offering descriptions that we understand to be true. It also provides techniques of normalisation, such as surveillance, measurement, categorisation, regulation and evaluation.
>
> (Dahlberg et al. 1999: 30)

The power enshrined in such dominant discursive regimes is evidenced by the way that practices can quickly be changed to 'fit' so-called legitimate requirements. This was very clearly demonstrated when the National Literacy Strategy was embraced (Bryan 2004; Hall 2004) and the speedy and almost unopposed thrust of synthetic phonics into what appears to be almost universal early literacy practice (Hynds 2007). Of course, confronting such apparently legitimate policies is an enormous challenge, and professionally risky, for teachers who themselves require support, nourishment and rewards in their professional lives. To partly counter the idea of confrontation or subversion, the idea of problematising thinking, of examining pedagogy, troubling over the dominant discourse and developing a 'critical dialogue' (Dahlberg *et al*. 1999: 139) has emerged from studies of Reggio Emilia, although perhaps not born in or confined to that practice.

Focusing professional engagement and children's valuable time on a somewhat blinkered approach to education and to learning will always be at the expense of other pedagogical choices. As Young argues, 'Where education is increasingly directed to political and economic goals and justified by them ... this instrumentalism necessarily reduces the space and autonomy for the work of specialist professionals' (2006: 20). There do seem, however, to be some small glimpses of hope for respect to be given to the zones of development that children themselves are motivated towards and consequently keen to reach. The teachers in this study appear to be spending their valuable time with children capitalising on opportunities to support and guide the creative, problem-solving, world-making, energetic and curious risk-takers which young children invariably are.

Summary

This chapter has created the conceptual framework within which research has been undertaken by:

- characterising the pedagogical context in early years education;
- identifying the potential for alternative practice and introducing the idea of affective, relational practice;
- considering the play discourse in policy in England and in EPPE and REPEY;
- discussing 'wittingness' and 'the plane of the personal' as opposed to an instrumental approach to education.

While government policy is creating a climate of compliance and urging teachers towards programmes of study focused single-mindedly on achieving pre-set national targets, there is evidence to suggest that this will not support children to develop and learn. There seems to be a need for an affective approach towards education that would allow the voices of both the children and their teachers to be heard. This will require more than simply new political rhetoric or re-branding of teaching professionals. It will require the teaching and learning landscape to be reconceptualised.

It is possible, however, to identify teachers and pedagogy in the early years of education that exist outside of a narrow standards framework and they may be described as intuitive and organic rather than instrumental and pre-ordained. In the following chapters, scholarship and research ranging across significant issues in the field will be identified in order to present a landscape of literature within which to set this study of early years teachers' narratives.

Chapter 2

Stories, storying and storytellers

This chapter attempts to honour work across different disciplines in order to unwrap some of the mystery surrounding apparently effective and affective teaching and learning. It is centred upon the belief that effectiveness is created by an emphasis upon strong interpersonal acts between teacher and learner, communicative acts which, while often initiated by learners (similar to the way that babies lead imitative acts, see Trevarthan's research 1998), are successfully developed by special adults. Such adults, including teachers, as I claim in this study, appear to be intuitive (Claxton 2000).

Human interactions and conversational opportunities have been seen as central to children's well-being and learning (McLean 1991). From the work of developmental scientists, neuroscience, sociology and other disciplines, strong arguments have combined to promote the significance of healthy and positive interactions in the early years of learning. Both Vygotsky (1978) and later Bruner (1986) emphasised the social nature of learning and the significance of the company of more knowledgeable others in creating a climate for learning and progression. Greenfield (2000) claims that conversation, regardless of material resources, matters to brain development and growth. Stated simply, interactions with people help to shape the brain. The research examining how babies think, helps to confirm that 'babies are especially tuned to people' and that the 'flirtatious dialogues' in which they engage with people they love result in them learning quickly (Gopnik *et al*. 1999: 95). Babies seem to come into the world already designed to learn from the people around them.

From the work of international research, then, the weight of evidence from across disciplinary fields is growing and is persuasive. Alongside this knowledge, it also seems evident that while some teachers persist in conventional instructional, often didactic pedagogies, some educators, in nurseries and schools, work in an intuitive and skilled manner, empathising successfully with children and fluently participating in and influencing children's narratives, their play and their learning. Such educators appear to create playful and conversational pedagogies, an approach clearly supported by research from different fields which claims that 'talk' matters to learning (Vygotsky 1978;

Bakhtin 1981; Bruner 1986; Rogoff 1990; Wertsch 1991). To accompany children in their play is a sophisticated role which may, as some suggest (see Gopnik 2009) be determined by biology. Thus, the intrinsic motivation of babies is mirrored by the intrinsic motivation of parents to share knowledge in a developmentally and culturally appropriate way. The intuitive behaviour defined by Claxton is underpinned by research to suggest that such ways of behaving with young children may in fact be biologically determined, and it is at the beginning of life as biology and culture entwine to create a sense of identity (Rogoff 1990) that an intuitive relationship is formed to support this development. While this may be a natural state between parents and children, it is possible to see how similar relationships can be created and nurtured by teachers of young children in their intimacy in play.

The story I want to tell is the story of playful professionals who play in spite of heavy prescription; those who are able to be professional in their approach while engaging at a deep level in the preferred activities of children and childhood. This engagement often, if not always, involves storying, co-constructing narratives with, next to, around and about children essentially for the children's purposes and for their pleasure. The additional narrative layer that I am including, the narratives of experience of such teachers, is articulated clearly later and takes a somewhat different approach in its emphasis on professional narratives as an information base, rather than the conventional 'othering' (Brown 2003) involved in previous studies. For example, Anning et al. identify as a significant theme 'developing a research discourse ... to encourage practitioners to challenge unverified rhetoric' (2004: 15), while this study enables two practitioners to themselves create the discourse.

There are several separate areas of research and literature to review, although there may be overlapping elements. The first will attempt to understand and define 'storying', this conscious act of interaction with young children; that is, the pedagogy undertaken in the classroom that involves adults and children sharing narratives. While other researchers have looked at the way that young children construct stories alone (see Barrs 1988; Fox 1988; David et al. 2000), I have chosen to focus upon communicative acts, reciprocal acts, engaging both adult and child. Working with young children involves the construction of narratives at many levels and sometimes in formal adult-led contexts. However, it is the 'storying' events that teachers and children often engage in informally and without preconstructed *visible* planning, and at many points of the day, that are distinctive in some practice and of particular interest. The co-construction of stories, oral narratives, during play presents significant occasions during which teaching and deliberate, yet invariably 'invisible' (Wood 1988) attempts to influence development occur. Understanding these occasions, their significance and their often, almost opportunist, nature will help to identify the games, the playfulness and the deep knowledge of those engaged. Issues of empathy, intimacy, trust and respect – attributes that may be visible in both teacher and learner – all appear to be central to such acts.

Understanding such a literacy event (Brice Heath 1983), the interactions and the nature of the discourse, will help to determine the power of the co-constructed narratives and their potential pedagogical impact. Addressing the relative importance of such storying occasions, relative that is to other literacy events that occur during the course of a typical school day, will help provide status for playful pedagogies. Why then are co-constructed storying events so important?

Understanding stories, storying and young storymakers

In order to understand the skills, knowledge and talents of young storymakers, and to respond to the questions of what occurs during storying interactions and why such storying events may be significant in learning, this section is divided into four key aspects. First, *world-making*, the importance of young children's amazing ability to develop and learn to construe their worlds in a relatively short time, initially in informal family and community con-texts, must be celebrated. Second, *conversations*, that is, the impact that con-versation has on children's knowledge and understanding of the world, which have now formed the essence of much research into early literacy development and will be significant to this study (Whitehead 1999a; Mercer 2000; Bearne 2002). Third, in the section on *story*, I argue that the ori-gins of story – stories, told, read and shared – form the bedrock of children's early learning and are a firm basis from which to create their own. And in the final section discussing *play* – pretend play, play as a site for drama – interaction and storying are considered the connecting element between home and school settings and as the place where storying events are most often embedded.

World-making

The importance of stories in children's emerging and developing under-standing of themselves, and themselves in relation to others and to the world, has been considered in a range of research spanning two or more decades (Britton 1970; Hardy 1977; Meek 1985; Barrs 1988; Rosen 1988). Rich descriptions in the literature illuminate how understanding, responding to story and constructing narrative have the power to engage children in making sense of their world (Whitehead 1997; David 1999; Abbott 2001; Bruce 2005). 'World-making' is a term widely used but rarely explained. In my study, world-making is used to refer to the ways in which children learn to view and construct themselves not only in relation to parents, family, friends and other community members, but also in relation to fixed states and artefacts. The 'tunes' and scenarios of family life during children's early development create the first dramas in which children participate and adopt roles as they learn to feed from the oral texts around them and contribute to them (Grainger *et al.* 2005). Bruner, in his work on narrative and story-making, claims that 'we constantly construct and reconstruct ourselves to meet the needs of the situations we encounter' (Bruner 2002: 64) and it has become evident, from a range of international research (David *et al.* 2003) that as early as in their second year of life babies are already able to construct 'pretend narratives' (ibid.: 58) to influence action and context. By the age of 3 and 4, children are demonstrating signs of a developing understanding of inner states (Dunn 1998). In Dunn's research (1998, 2004), this is referred to as mind reading. She examines how, as children become less preoccupied with immediate desires or needs, they are able to engage in pretend or imaginary worlds with, predominantly, their mothers, which Dunn describes as a sophisticated and cognitively demanding act. Parents, carers, siblings, friends, community members all contribute to the dramatic setting into which children are born and grow. It is in such social settings that children develop attachments, learn hierarchies, understand values and develop a sense of self, of who they are and their place in this small world in which they find themselves. This selfhood seems to develop and to be derived from experiences in the company of significant others – in relationships. Trevarthan talks about children's 'essential motivation' as striving 'to comprehend the world by sharing experiences and purposes with other minds' (1998: 87) and in this way family and community values and cultural understandings develop.

From this cultural background children learn to relate beyond their immediate community to the wider world, while continuing to glance back to make referential connections that make sense to them and thus construct a world-view. As children puzzle and struggle to make sense of the physical and conceptual world of home and family, they are able to increasingly demonstrate control over the spaces they inhabit, the artefacts around them and their physical environment as well as developing relationships (Cole 1998). The strength or otherwise of these early foundations seems to determine future growth, and research is now gathering pace to support the notion that early loving interactions affect cognitive growth and development (Gopnik *et al.* 1999; Gerhardt 2004; David 2007). Communicative acts, ways of expressing their developing understandings and sense of self build 'on the values and the understanding of the world acquired in a long history of culturally constituted experience' (Super and Harkness 1998: 45). While some of the most recent studies have gathered strength and credibility through their employment of contemporary breakthroughs in technology (see, for example, the work of cognitive science and neuro-science in Greenfield 2000; Meltzoff 2002; Blakemore and Frith 2005), Mead's seminal sociological theories, at the beginning of the last century, portrayed very similar ideas, that minds should be seen as 'phenomena which have arisen and developed out of the process of communication and of social experience generally' (in Carreira da Silva 2007: 39). Indeed, the essence of Paolo Freire's extensive and passionate work in relation to literacy learning is that 'reading the world always precedes reading the word' (Freire and Macedo 1987: 35). In view of these arguments, it seems that a curriculum founded upon social experience, particularly in the early years of education is essential.

Conversations

At home, then, babies and children learn to engage with natural curiosity and enthusiasm in co-constructed narratives, often play narratives, with family members as they build and make sense of an enculturated world and their place in it (Grainger *et al*. 2005). In combinations of everyday activities, conversations and play, young children's narratives form part of an 'apprenticeship of thinking' (Mercer 2000: 132) as they grow up in families and communities. A range of 'cognitively rich conversations' (Dunn 1998) take place during everyday events (see also Wells 1986). As children affectively engage in authentic experiences, live their lives, in the culture-rich company of others, talk is a key feature: to question, explain, define, describe, challenge, defend, express love, disagree, to account for action, narrate, mediate, report, instruct, and so on. While it is clear that 'people living in different parts of the world and at different times hold diverse beliefs about the nature and nurturing of infants' (DeLoache and Gottlieb 2000: 2), it is also without doubt that human infants are 'special' in their 'utter reliance on sustained and extended interaction with a committed and enculturated caregiver' (Bruner 2000: ix).

We (adults and children) 'appropriate' ways of using language from those around us (Mercer 2000; Carter 2004) and so find our own voice. Young children can often be heard trying out sounds, tunes, patterns, accents and manners of expression and in informal talk contexts adults are able to help to 'further develop ripening functions' (Geekie *et al*. 1999: 16). Carter refers to 'everyday creativity' in his close examination of conversation and considers how 'ordinary' language can be 'pervasively unordinary' in interactive and interpersonal discourse (2004: 24). Word play, the creation of private family language, subversive play with language (Grainger and Goouch 1999) form the bedrock of children's early language learning as children develop as symbolisers (Vygotsky 1978) – learning to symbolically play with ideas and meanings. Children in home contexts are guided in 'casual, incidental ways as adults and children go about their joint activities' (Mercer 2000: 135) in their everyday lives, without thought of instruction or causal learning opportunities. This kind of 'transparent' teaching (Wells 1986; Wood 1988), also challenged by Bernstein (1997: 61) as 'invisible pedagogy', has been amply described and analysed.

Mercer's (2000) term 'interthinking' helps to create a picture of adults and children puzzling to make sense together – a more equitable role than instructor and learner and with children's intentions at the forefront. Adults, sensitive to children's intentions in play and functional acts, are said in this way to 'scaffold' children's learning in conversational contexts. This metaphor of a 'scaffold' is often overused and mistakenly taken to represent a preconstructed, upright, rigid structure – intending to reach a single destination, or objective. Of course, the critical question then would be, what or where next? Grenfell (Grenfell and James 1998) refers to the scaffolding metaphor as a utilitarian construct which is of course troublesome in the kind of organic learning context of home and family. However, Matthews describes an observation of scaffolding somewhat differently, with sensitivity and deep understanding of the subtle and sophisticated nature of teaching and learning. The following vignette from Matthews' work is rich in meaning:

> When Kingsley lifts the column up he notices me video recording him and looks at me, wondering perhaps what I am doing and he forgets building. His building block is held, now forgotten, just above his shoulder. Hwee Huang gently coaxes his building arm downward with a subtle brush of her hand, her fingers fanning over first his forearm and then, without pausing in their downward path, his leg. This gesture is like a gentle wave motion washing over him. It is the lightest of caresses, almost without weight, like a butterfly alighting upon him, yet it is dense with meaning. She is trying to nudge him back onto his course – a course which she interiorizes, perhaps inferring it from his actions and constructing it in her own mind, and which she helps him sustain.
>
> This is what Jerome Bruner (1964) means by 'scaffolding'. It is not to be understood simply as a physical process; it involves a psychological empathy with the child and an understanding of what he or she might be moving toward. Nor is it a one-way process from the teacher to the child. When it exists, it is a fluid, dynamic and often seemingly effortless dance between teacher and child.
>
> (Matthews 1999: 162)

This level of interaction, 'nudging' children rather than directing them, is closer to the principles discussed in this study and also close to the nature of early learning at home. It suggests a very close, intimate connection between the adult and child, with each understanding the other's intentions and actions but without recourse necessarily, in this example, to spoken language. Wordless conversations such as the one described above are important in the depth of 'interthinking' that is required and involves the cultural understandings of gesture and touch.

Conversation used as a site for learning is not a novel idea in any universal sense but may often be considered less seriously in print-dominated and target and standards-dominated teaching cultures. It is possible to find teachers who simply do not converse with children in their care in their classrooms (Bennett 1976; Wells 1986). However; conversation is deeply significant in learning and in education (Wells 1986; Greenfield 2000; Carter 2004). Conversation may be used to evidence development and so the claim that 'conversational intelligence is the hallmark of a human mind ... an intelligence that tries to navigate with other minds to share the process of conscious awareness and purposeful thinking' (Trevarthan 1998: 90) could be a considerable influence on current primary pedagogies. This kind of activity as a measure of intelligence would require some radical rethinking of school-based education, which currently only measures intelligence through subject-based performance in examination contexts and would perhaps need a reconceptualisation of what society needs and understands in relation to both school and education before it is possible (see the arguments posited by Noddings in her critique of Liberal Education theories 1992: 28).

Mercer's research, undertaken over almost two decades, is highly significant in understanding children's cultural social and cognitive development through shared talk. He describes how children are able to link intellects as their 'individual development is shaped by their dialogues with the people around them' (2000: 11). The myth that young children simply absorb information like a sponge is contestable and the seminal works of Tizard and Hughes (1984) and Wells (1986) describe young children as 'puzzlers' who are busy putting collected data together, from conversational sources, to answer their questions of the world. This theory fits appropriately with the work from neuro-science which suggests that from birth babies are active learners, often leading 'conversation' and interaction and making connections. Babies are born to learn and, as Gopnik claims, 'Babies' brains seem to have special qualities that make them especially well suited for imagaination and learning. Babies brains are actually more highly connected than adult brains; more neural pathways are available to babies than adults' (Gopnik 2009: 11).

In his research with older children, Mercer examines how collaboration is an effective human activity as teachers and learners combine mental resources in conversation. He develops this idea here:

> Human communication partners need not just take what the other gives and then go and carry out individual activities, as do the honey bees; they can use information which has been shared as an intellectual resource, working on it to make better sense than they might alone.
>
> (Mercer 2000: 172)

His discussions of 'communities of discourse' and 'specialised discourse' can be equally applied to the play contexts of young children as they can to more easily identifiable learning contexts of older children and adults. And Mercer's 'discourse guides' can include both parents, siblings and other family and community members as well as those working with children in early years settings. Indeed, in play, the 'relationship between talk and the physical environment and other semiotic systems' (i.e. gesture and drawing) (ibid.: 23) is easily visible as children naturally use everything that they have to hand to make meanings explicit (Kress 1997; Pahl 1999). Mercer's idea of 'intermental perspectives' is particularly apposite in this study of children's and teachers' co-constructed narratives, as each understand and work together to achieve a joint action. This idea of 'shared intellectual resources' is often very apparent on the occasions when adults and children, often small children, work together to make sense of what is happening, as they create stories.

Story

From early gestures and simple communicative acts in infancy to the construction of complex story narratives in early childhood, literacy encompasses major chunks of children's lives in their first years. Within this, stories told, made, thought, dreamt, found, drawn, written or read, all implicitly or overtly surround us before birth onwards. Although some traditionalists bemoan the fact that parents often neglect reading stories to children, contemporary story encounters may be differently constructed, for example, on screen, on DVDs or on computer games. Indeed, some advertisers now use the story genre on television and advertising hoardings to send their messages, knowing that children and their families are accustomed to finding metaphor and analogy in such narratives.

Story has often been said, crudely, to provide an escape from reality or alternatively to mirror the real world. However, Bruner (2002) has some suggestions to make. His arguments are rather more subtle but also suggest a substantially more active role for story and response to story. He suggests that 'fictional narrative gives shape to things in the real world and often bestows on them a title to reality' (ibid.: 8) but also that it makes 'the familiar and the ordinary strange again' (ibid.: 9) and that it 'offers alternative worlds that put the actual one in a new light' (ibid.: 10). Bruner also subtly challenges the notion that 'the story form is a transparent window on reality' but rather 'a cookie cutter imposing a shape on it' (ibid.: 6, 7).

In these terms, young children are expert cookie cutters in their story constructions, weaving together the familiar and the strange, the imagined and the lived to denote new realities in the real world of play. Making sense of themselves and their world and their place within it seems to be the central function and focus of children's play, most often highly visible in their socio-dramatic play. And so if, as Bruner claims, 'we constantly construct and reconstruct our selves to meet the needs of the situations we encounter, and we do so with the guidance of our memories of the past and our hopes and fears for the future', then the very beginnings and development of this can be seen in the story constructions of children in play (see also the work of Bettelheim 1978, 1982).

The centrality of story in our lives is better understood if it is possible to stand back and reflect on everyday occasions when 'story' is experienced. In any context of human encounters – homes, coffee shops, bars, hairdressers, buses, school gates, staff rooms – a range of story narratives can be heard, including excuses, fabrications, complaints, anecdote, gossip, tales and conversation. These combine to make up huge and fundamental portions of our lives. Rosen claims that 'the drive to represent experiences as narrative is indestructible' (1988: 9).

He explains that:

> So it is that we can readily conceive of ourselves as deprived of all kinds of cultural resources, TV, theatres, even books, but strip us of all the accumulation of stories, heard and told, reported and invented, traditional and spontaneous and what is left of us?
>
> (ibid.: 8)

Rosen discusses stories as a 'product of the predisposition of the human mind to narrativise experience and to transform it into findings which as social beings we may share and compare with those of others' (ibid.: 12). And now, in a time with almost universal access to mobile phones, talk, conversation and general narratives surround and sometimes deafen us as experiences can instantly be shared with the support of technology. Making stories, making meaning and world-making have been described as being fundamental to human existence (Bruner 1986, 2002; Rosen 1988). We create, embellish, dramatise, inherit and bequeath stories that map and define our place in the world. Stories are used to mediate our culture and cultural practices, to pass on values and traditions and to initiate and shape the knowledge, understandings, belief and behaviour of new entrants into families and communities.

The additional dimension of computer technology as well as influences from television, screen literacy, has also to be added to this wide-ranging and rich picture of early story practices across many cultures and communities (Kenner 2004). Children's cultural induction to story includes access to whatever family and community practices allow in relation to multimedia. Very young children are introduced to conventional forms of story from oral tales and print versions as well as through more visual texts on screens varying from small hand-held toys specifically designed for young users, television stories, videos, virtual worlds specifically designed for them and often associated with commercial artifacts (see Marsh 2005) and then to the PlayStations suited to older children, as well as adult-oriented computer games and film (Kress 1997, 2000; Marsh and Millard 2000). Theoretically, this range should enlarge the repertoire of children's stories, and it is possible to see in practice how this occurs and how popular cultural texts feed and resource children's own storymaking (Marsh and Millard 2000; Bearne 2003; Lambirth 2003) and how media and other textual references frequently appear in children's play designs. Comic strip heroes, for example, are a common feature of playground play.

Play

It is difficult to see, in one sense, how play can be separated from 'world-making', 'conversation' and 'story', as, very often, all are drawn together in play. While it is important to acknowledge their interdependency and co-existence, play itself always requires some discussion of definition and boundaries and needs to be clearly set within research domains to enable its very existence to be firmly justified. While this is not a study of play, nor claiming to be a review of literature in the field of play, any consideration of young children's learning would be remiss if it excluded literature that attempted to understand the place of play in children's lives and learning. Indeed, play has been described as 'the signature of childhood' (Gopnik 2009: 14). One of the key founding principles of play, unequivocally stated by Bruce, is that 'children choose to play, they cannot be made to play' (2005: 132) and this will underpin all subsequent discussions of play in this study.

Careful observations of babies and their mothers or caregivers have demonstrated how play is the child's world as they absorb, search and explore the peopled environment of their home. Mothers become a baby's first 'plaything' and predominantly, as primary caregivers, their prime 'playmate' (Newson and Newson 1979: 39). By the age of six months, babies' body activities have developed a new vigour and variety (Trevarthan 1998) as they develop more control, and playful expressions, playful teasing and playful companionships become part of the repertoire of their routine activities. Trevarthan also points to the 'innate musicality' and 'poetic and musical awareness' that he believes are part of the non-verbal abilities possessed by all humans which helps them to 'interact mentally and make sense of one another's feelings, actions, ideas and opinions' (ibid.: 92). This 'unconscious level of communication' (ibid.: 92) in playful, culturally understood contexts will underpin future interactive storying events in other settings.

Play, though, particularly as children move beyond infancy, is a contested space and crosses boundaries of research disciplines as efforts are made to understand both its nature and its uses. The term 'play' is used widely and differently, for example, playing with (someone or something), playing around, playing games, playing at (someone or something) all suggest a recreational or leisure activity. Indeed, the expression 'fooling around' is often substituted, which serves to further denigrate the activity towards the 'carnivalesque', although some researchers relish this association, particularly in relation to risky language play (see, for example, Grainger and Goouch 1999: 24).

In Figure 2.1, Moyles has identified themed research connections to theories of play and has demonstrated the range of potentially interested research disciplines.

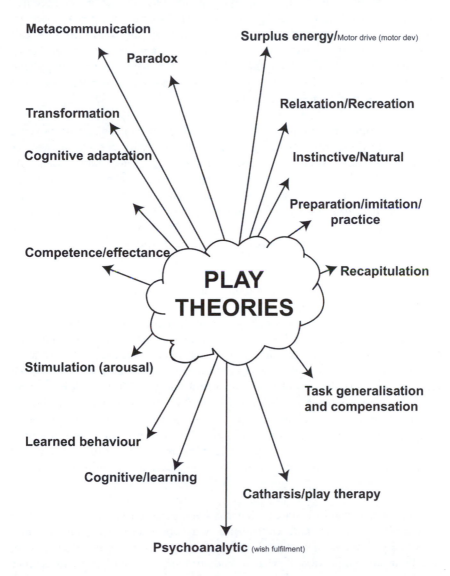

Figure 2.1 Play theories
Source: Adapted from Moyles (2005a: 5)

While it is important on occasion to validate play by attempts to understand its importance and connections to the wider world of thinking and
learning, the challenge with this way of looking at play is that *children's* play
can then be hijacked in order to fulfil other intentions. For example, the
cognitive applications described above are often used to account for the existence of play in education settings. Drummond describes this as 'the benevolent
educator's attempt to kidnap the spontaneity of play for a pre-specified
learning objective' (2001: x). However, it is also worth noting that there are
clear advantages to creating dynamic and far-reaching connections of this
nature as the status of play may be significantly increased by such interests,
particularly in political circles, although its integrity may suffer in the process.
Historically, in the political domain, play has consistently been considered to
be of very low status, as Anning relates:

> A few comments from [their] public announcements ... will serve to
> illustrate the point. Michael Fallon, a Minister with the Department of
> Education and Science, criticising the use of project work, said: 'At
> worst this kind of practice turns the primary school into playgroups
> where there is much happiness and painting but very little learning.'
> Kenneth Clarke, in a brief period of opportunism, claimed that 'child-
> centred' education was 'failing to deliver: At its weakest there is a lot of
> sticking together of egg boxes and playing in the sand.'
>
> (1994: 17)

And of course these kinds of comments clearly indicate the lack of political
understanding in learning at all.

Clear definitions of play are hard to find. Jenkinson describes play as
'embrac[ing] children's total experience ... play is not ordered and rational'
(2001: 42), which perhaps explains why it is so hard to contain and to measure
by conventional means within a structured curriculum and why it is often
dominated by the rhetoric of progress (Sutton-Smith 1997) as adults seek to
justify its very existence in children's lives. Just as adults play – 'plays are
play and so are novels, paintings and songs', so too in childhood play is 'a
living, visible manifestation of imagination and learning in action' (Gopnik
2009: 14). In her description of play, Bruce creates an explanation that would
probably make it even less palatable to the government ministers quoted
above:

> Play is about wallowing in what has been experienced and dealing with
> mastering, facing and controlling what is experienced emotionally,
> socially, bodily, in movement, thoughts and ideas. It is, in the main,
> about the application of what is known, using the skill and competence
> that has been developed.
>
> (Bruce 1994: 265)

The work of neuro-science helps a little in debates about the worth of play by describing how prolific the expansion of synaptic connections is in the very early stages of an infant's life, emphasising too the plasticity of the brain (Sutton-Smith 1997; Greenfield 2000). Play offers the great opportunity for infants and young children to exploit their brain's potential, to shape their own brain, through the myriad of opportunities that arise in such contexts. Young children's ambition, their failure to see boundaries, the ways in which they 'overestimate their ability to function skilfully' (Sutton-Smith 1997: 226), their risk-taking and risky behaviour, their attempts to become 'a head taller than themselves' (Vygotsky 1978: 102) all contribute to the brain shaping that appears to occur and to the 'actualisation of those potential neural connections' which are 'especially well epitomised by play' (Sutton-Smith 1997: 227).

In view of arguments of this kind to support the need for children to play, and for play, and indeed learning, to be volitional, the real debate is how much of their time should children spend *not* playing, rather than whether children should play, and also how much of their time *in educational settings* should children not be playing. While it may be evident that play is not the only way in which children learn, and that children engage in other activities that are 'good', it does seem that it needs to be 'at the heart' of children's experiences (Bruce 1994: 266), reinforcing their zestfulness, rather than marginalised to corners of 'golden time', a practice of rewarding children with play for other performance achievements (Lambirth and Goouch 2006). Inevitably, then, teachers of young children would need to become involved in play, observers of play, authors or co-authors of play contexts, players themselves and in this way to be able to both understand play and to participate in play, as will be further discussed in relation to the practice of the two teachers in this study. Play, and zestfulness, are contagious if we only let them into our lives, or at least our professional lives.

Pretend play

Although this should not be seen as separate from play itself, pretend play does deserve a special mention in the context of the practice and pedagogy later discussed. It is in her work definitively describing why stories and narratives matter in our lives and why children quickly become attuned to and adept at storying that Whitehead helps explain why children engage in this kind of activity (1997). She confirms that the development of memory, the need to recall and retell events and the need to organise our existence, all contribute to the way we make sense of the world through narrative expression. Put simply, she explains that 'all this ordering, explaining and evaluating that goes on in narratives is a way of giving meaning and significance to the endless stream of sensations and events' (ibid.: 90). She further states that the most important urge we have is to hold on to and 'repeat or represent for consideration what was in actuality a transient happening, giving it shape and pattern and, consequently some kind of meaning or significance' (ibid.: 90) and thus makes sense of the continuous and repetitious actions of children in play as they re-play and re-rehearse their lived lives, which is sometimes not 'fun' but nevertheless crucial (see, for example, Steedman's seminal text *The Tidy House* 1982).

In the context of children's play, in particular, fantasy play, pretend play, role play or socio-dramatic play – all versions of the same play space – young children have the opportunity to re-live, re-present and re-shape their own lived experiences. Relationships and events can all be recalled, revisited (or not), retained and refined or simply retold. In the kind of play described here, the teller controls and shapes the action and sequences events and predicts outcomes. The creation of play narratives, or storying, is a way for young children to make visible what is in 'their mind's eye' or their 'mind's ear' as they reflect upon their world, their families, relationships and their own place in it all. Children seem naturally to be 'wild pretenders' (Gopnik 2009: 73), an apt term to describe the abandon, the commitment and the physicality often apparent in children's pretend play. It is a tradition borne over centuries and embedded in oral traditions from across cultures and communities (Grainger 1997; Whitehead 1997). Symbolism in such narratives operates at more than one level as children quickly draw on objects and artefacts to 'stand for' people, places and things, but they are also able to symbolise the very event being recalled and draw on metaphors to support them. Children, in their naïve sophistication, are able to dovetail stories within stories, interweave the entire range of significant people in their lives in their tales and create complex intertextual narratives over time (Whitehead 1997; David *et al.* 2000). In creating, co-creating and recreating stories in this way, children seem to be able to solve puzzles from their lives or preserve moments in time that matter. Stories created and told in play are closely connected to children's developing selfhood (Whitehead 1997; Egan 2003), an idea that leads Whitehead to claim that 'if we are to some extent what we know about ourselves, we are also a created fiction' (Whitehead 1997: 94). In a description of how the stages of play help children in their development of self, Mead explains how play supports the principle of 'taking the attitude of the other' and how, 'by learning to play at being something other than they are, children begin to acquire a structured self ... an object of [their] own experience' (Carreira da Silva 2007: 48). Play is also highly speculative and tentative as children are continually reconstructing the space, asking 'what if ... ' questions of themselves and others and constructing new, possibly fictive, solutions and endless possibilities in their play scenarios. Participating in this kind of play as an adult requires sophisticated skills of narrative construction, collaboration, cooperation, the ability to listen, to co-construct, to empathise, to courageously take on roles and to be led by children, and requires also that they actively give time, physical and conceptual space and status to play. Participating in play is complex and requires a special kind of adult and very special and trusting relationships.

Chapter 3

Playful teachers, playful pedagogies
Intuition, relationships and ideologies

An assumption of this study is that some adults can be described as 'intuitive' in their actions (Atkinson and Claxton 2000). Who are the teachers who can teach in this way? Do all intuitive teachers of children in the early years of education 'story' with children? Deconstructing the identity of intuitive teachers will require an understanding of the values they may hold, their perceptions and their ideologies and an understanding of their sense of professional identity. A number of questions arise in relation to identity and teaching. For example, what is the strength of the relationship that exists between the teacher and their values, including ideology, particularly in view of the strength of current political imperatives? What is s/he embracing in her/his practice and, importantly, what is s/he rejecting? (Are you what you teach?) Developing a construction of 'professionals' and 'professionalism' is particularly important currently when such constructs are open for public and political debate and are often contentious. Definitions of these terms are especially important in the field of early years education as training, qualifications and self-esteem vary between those adults working with young children. Who then has claim to the badge of 'professional' and who has the power to define such terms?

Attempts to understand the complexities of human relationships, teaching and learning interactions and the nature of co-constructed narratives invariably cross boundaries of subject domains. These may include studies from psychology in relation to personality, identity and selfhood; from sociology considering, for example, theories of the primacy of society over individuals (Durkheim 1956), of the use of teachers as technicians to serve society's needs (Woods and Jeffrey 2004), of the significance of national policies in the lives of teachers; and from education, the business of professionals and pedagogies. This collected wisdom from across disciplines and from theorists and researchers may help the smallest children in our educational systems to learn, affectively and effectively – if that is the intention.

Further, there is also a socio-political view to consider, that is that political intentions in relation to schooling may be rather more connected with social control than liberation and empowerment, bound to the development of functional literacy rather than creative freedoms, tied to conventional, short-term national objectives rather than visionary, personal aims (Ball 2004). Evidence of this can be seen in contemporary curricula redesigned to include, for example, citizenship, and in examples of 'creative compliance' (Lambirth and Goouch 2006) where small attempts are made to conform to both a standards-led curriculum and new creativity initiatives, but still tied securely to crudely defined assessment tools (see Halpin and Troyna 1994). However the national picture is viewed, there still remains the personal dimension, that is, that all 'school' learning occurs in a social context. It is dependent upon relationships, reciprococity and language (Bruner 1986; Rogoff 1990; Shotter 1993; Carter 2004). Power structures are such in educational settings that the shape of those relationships, the potential for reciprocal events and the nature of language employed, are all within the control of one individual, the teacher, in spite of prescriptive pedagogies. Unwrapping then the teacher's values, intentions, ideology and drive seems crucial to understanding the potential for children and their learning in such an individual's care.

Who are the teachers who can engage with children in co-constructing play narratives in informal, play contexts without hijacking the event? Who are the educators who understand the significance of such events and give status to these opportunities? Human encounters (McLean 1991) matter in education and there appears to be only a core of special educators working in the system who understand and respect the intentionality of children and have, as a fundamental part of their teaching repertoire, the ability to intuitively respond and engage with children's created narratives. Intuition in practice has been described as the way in which 'explicit knowledge and implicit "know-how" are braided together in professional contexts' (Atkinson and Claxton 2000: 3). Deconstructing or unbraiding the nature of the explicit and tacit or implicit knowledge exposes the strength and sophistication of home learning before formal schooling begins and of the work of those other than formally qualified 'teachers' in enabling development. Powerful learning takes place in a comparatively short time scale from birth to school starting age when children encounter formal teaching. The significance of the familiarity of the context, the physical environment and the strength of the relationships contribute to this deep learning. Indeed, Dunn reminds us that there are 'crucial differences in children's communicative and reflective behaviour at home – in the context of a supportive mother–child relationship, and at school, where all too often the adult–child interaction did not have this quality of supportive interest' (Dunn 1998: 90). There is little evidence, except in isolated cases to be explored later, that Dunn's research findings are any less relevant in current school settings. There is, however, strong evidence that the reverse is true (Anning 2004) and that teachers, even in the early years of education, may be becoming 'technicians' to fulfil the requirements of politicians here in the UK, who also seem to meet the current expectations of society in general, or at best are 'walking on two legs' (Dahlberg et al. 1999) and engaging in 'strategic compliance' (Lacey 1977, cited in Woods and Jeffrey 2004: 236). Teachers, who are in public service, are in rather a difficult position unless there is some unified attempt to make clear the aims of what we all understand to be 'education' in school and other institutional contexts.

Defining education

Superficially, at least, Durkheim's writing at the turn of the last century in France where the church and the state were rivals for influence in education, will resonate with some of the political initiatives here in the UK at the end of the last century and the beginning of this. He defines education in a not dissimilar way to recent government education initiatives (Stannard 1999; Department for Education and Skills, 2006), claiming the primacy of society over the individual:

> Education is the influence exercised by adult generations on those that are not yet ready for social life. Its object is to arouse and to develop in the child a certain number of physical, intellectual and moral states which are demanded of him by both the political society as a whole and the special mileu for which he is specially destined.
>
> (Durkheim 1956: 71)

In contrast, Pring uses the metaphor of 'emancipation' for education as opposed to 'enslavement' born of ignorance and discusses the idea that 'to be educated' means that you have the skills, abilities and disposition to make sense of the world. But he travels even further with this idea and maintains that education is broader than only 'making sense of that which is inherited from others' but instead education 'gives access to the ideas, and thus the tools, through which the learner's own distinctive personal development might actively take place' (Pring 2004: 27). Such a philosophical view is itself in direct contrast to the current, rather more utilitarian, ideology represented in current statutory curriculum requirements and presents challenges to teachers who limit themselves to the achievement of prescribed objectives. There is currently in evidence an 'ideology of control' (Noddings 1992: 62); control of content, control of performance criteria, control of behaviour and control of documentation, all of which is centrally defined and centrally monitored. It then becomes very difficult for individual teachers to move beyond this and towards a more collaborative and community-based pedagogy as in, for example, New Zealand, where Te Whariki is built upon consensus and cultural acknowledgement (see the work of May 2002 for a fuller consideration of New Zealand politics, history and policy).

Taking the individual out of the education equation in the utilitarian way described above has been challenged by research in other disciplines since the early twentieth century. The nature of education has been redefined, as in

Freire's writing, where he claims education to be 'an act of love and thus an act of courage' (1976: 38) personalising teaching and recreating education as a domain where individuals are significant. He appeals for learning 'from the inside out' in collaboration with educators and asserts that '[education] is not the transference of knowledge, but the encounter of subjects in dialogue in search of the significance of knowing and thinking' (ibid.: 143). This kind of collaborative thinking relates closely to my interpretation of Mercer's 'intermental' perspectives, cited earlier. Reconstructing education in this way forefronts ideas about communities of learning and rearranges roles of powerful adults and powerless learners into more equitable collaborative, co-constructed spaces. Freire describes a class as 'a meeting place where knowledge is sought and not where it is transmitted' (ibid.: 148). The practice that Freire promotes, where children are agents of their own learning, is close in nature to that apparently taking place in Reggio Emilia pre-schools in Northern Italy. In this district, the pre-schools operate a pedagogy of relationships (Rinaldi 2005) and create communities of practice (Wenger 1998) where the shared discourse focuses upon children's intentions and their sustained intellectual engagement, in the company of others.

Wenger's argument in relation to the development of 'communities of practice' is that learning is more than merely the acquisition of skills and information; he describes it as a lifelong process, 'a process of becoming ... an experience of identity' because it transforms who we are and what we are able to do' (1998: 215). Wenger also seeks to redefine the roles and nature of 'teachers' because of the danger that 'the pedagogical and institutional functions of educators [may] displace their ability to manifest their identities as participants in their communities of practice, [and so] they may lose their most powerful teaching asset' (ibid.: 276). His suggestion is that for effective learning, adults should just be adults, rather than taking the institutional role of educator, 'who are willing to invite [children] into adulthood' (ibid.: 277) and this connects closely to the work of at least one of the two teachers described later, whose description of himself fits neatly into Wenger's ideas of effective adults. The mutuality of engagement and interactive learning then creates ease of participation but is completely dependent on the security of the adults involved in their own knowledge of theories of learning, pedagogy and development and their trust in children as learners. In this radical redefinition of teacher/educator, Wenger goes further to argue that: 'It is the learning of mature members and of their communities that invites the learning of newcomers. As a consequence, it is as learners that we become educators' (ibid.: 277). The importance of mentors, in Wenger's terms, becomes significant to this work and is further explored in later chapters.

'Community' is an interesting term and who teachers are, in relation to the communities in which they practise, may be significant. For example, Rogoff claims that in some communities young children are not expected to interact as equals with adults and any attempt to be a 'conversational peer' would not be acceptable (Rogoff *et al.* 1998: 235). Equally, power principles of talk practice may also be a tradition in which teachers have grown and developed, causing them to create only unequal participation, where power structures are clearly defined. Thus, the values and cultural practices of both educators and communities need to be clearly understood. Where, how and in what political context teachers are themselves educated, as pupils and as student teachers, influence their pedagogy as well as the policies from which they currently practise. A key element in the practice of Reggio Emilia pre-schools is the reflective discourse in which all engage, which enables implicit know-how and understandings to become publicly articulated, debated and documented. This practice is, however, unusual except possibly where the Reggio Emilia sphere of influence has travelled, for example, in Stockholm (Dahlberg *et al.* 1999). More commonly, as in discussions of Bourdieu's sociological stance on education and practice, 'the defining principles are only ever partially articulated, and much of the orthodox way of thinking and acting passes on in an implicit, tacit manner' (Grenfell and James 1998: 20). The sociological and ideological stance of teachers is deeply significant in their pedagogical choices and their influences then must be worthy of close examination. Bourdieu's theories of 'capital' – social, economic and cultural capital – connect closely with Brice Heath's seminal ethnographic study of the communities of literacy practice in and around a town in the recently desegregated south of the United States (Brice Heath 1983). Brice Heath discovered that, as in Bourdieu's writing, those children whose life and cultural identity 'most resembles the cultural dispositions, and hence values, through which the school seeks to work [the legitimate] are more likely to be disposed to a certain type of practice through a process of elective affinities' (Bourdieu, cited in Grenfell and James, 1998: 21).

There are, of course, visible and invisible 'operations' at play in school interactions (Bernstein 1997) and these are invariably influenced and constructed by the cultural and pedagogical 'knowing' of teachers as well as the politically driven policies of the moment.

Bourdieu's theory that 'culture attracts culture', which seems to be almost indisputable, is interesting in relation particularly to young children, whose predispositions and behaviours often tend to fly in the face of theoretical understanding. It is gratifying to remember the overwhelming competence of small children in their energetic and insatiable desire to learn and that one of their most significant and universal talents is in their ability to attract collaborators in their learning journeys. By the age of 2, children's intersubjectivity is said to be both 'rich and subtle' and 'they communicate in ways that bring their consciousness and understandings together' (Trevarthan 1998: 95). By the time children are between the ages of 3 and 4, immediately before school age in the UK, 'they will have become accomplished collaborators with siblings or peers as well as adults. They will also have become adept in switching between the roles of learner, play partner and increasingly, of "teacher" as

well' (Woodhead *et al.* 1998: 5–6), and their choices of role partners and collaborators often defy prediction. Indeed, small children are said to have increasing
'tenacity in the pursuit of social contact' (Bronfenbrenner 1972: 294). The
ways that teachers respond to such tenacity are informed by their values and
beliefs, which may or may not coincide with current education policy, but
which will always fall in the continuum ranging from intuitive human
response to coercive institutional practitioner.

Influential authors and educators in the field of early education, including
Froebel in the nineteenth century and Montessori in the early twentieth century (Bruce 1987; Nutbrown *et al.* 2008), have particularly emphasised the
respectful relationship between educator and learner and, recently, the work
of Malaguzzi in Reggio Emilia has pursued this idea of a 'pedagogy of relationships' (Rinaldi 2005). However, the current prevailing politics of education, and subsequent policy in England, challenge research and educational
philosophy which questions whether schools are becoming 'monasteries or
market places' (Menter *et al.* 1997; Pring 2004), with the implication that
market forces, competition and globalised economic realities influence constructions of both childhood and schooling. In his use of metaphorical language
here, Pring is also concerned that teaching has been reduced to curriculum
delivery rather than 'an engagement with other minds' (Pring 2004: 68). It
would, however, require deep commitment and courage to challenge prevailing
doctrine and many decades of accepted practice.

In her sensitively reported enquiry into the interpretative practice of early
years educators, McLean argues that the 'internal aspects of the person who is
the teacher (self-concept, beliefs about learning and teaching, awareness of own
biography)' connect with the physical environment and subsequent teacher
behaviour will be 'complex, reflexive and multi-directional' (McLean 1991:
7). She argues that teacher belief and action are bound together in complex
ways, although this study, while acknowledging the complexities, assumes
them to be inseparable.

I am what I teach

In a detailed study of primary school teachers, Nias explores the nature of
'teachers' selves'. She gathers research support for the notion that 'we each
develop a relatively impervious "substantial self" which can be distinguished
from our "situational selves" and which incorporates those beliefs, values and
attitudes which we feel to be most self-defining' (Nias 1989: 21). Her analysis
of interviews with teachers further indicates that 'the personal values which
are incorporated in individual's substantial selves play an important part in the
way they conceptualize and carry out their work' (ibid.: 41). The 'fusion' that
Nias encounters, of personal and occupational self-image, supports the idea
that the values that teachers hold, which may not be static but dynamic and
evolving, substantially influence pedagogical possibilities. However, there are

new theories and discourse in relation to 'managerialism', particularly in the UK but also in other English-speaking countries. These theories make claims of a connection between managerial control and issues of quality (Olssen *et al.* 2004), with accompanying obsessions with objectives and quality audits. Such obsessions may rather overwhelm other contemporary theories relating to personal engagement and a pedagogical discourse centred on relationships. Audit accountability is becoming the power that weakens teachers' personal engagement and investment in educational practice as they struggle with prescriptive practice and attempts to redefine teacher identity. Woods and Jeffrey go further to claim that 'the personal identity of work has become a situational one, designed to meet the instrumental purposes of audit accountability' (2004: 238).

The current dominant discourse, which includes attention to education markets and audits, leaves little room for interpretative responses and personal interaction and is a far cry from Freire's definition of education as an act of love. Pollard, however, returns the discussion to the idea of the child as agent of their own learning, suggesting that learning 'requires conditions which enable each child to control the assembly and construction of their understanding' (Pollard 2004: 294). He introduces the idea of teachers as 'reflective agents' in children's learning which depends on a 'sensitivity and accurate knowledge of each child's needs' (ibid.: 295).

The challenge, and it seems to be a challenge of magnitude, is to see how current political and societal expectations of teachers, influencing *their* self-concepts and identity, combined with published policy and purposes for education, can in any way relate to sociological and socio-cultural understandings of learners' identity and development in educational settings. Or indeed, whether political, societal or policy-makers' expectations filter through at all in any real way to teachers' lived professional lives.

Playful pedagogy

There are of course concerns when a government catches up with public concern and takes an interest in an idea, a sector of society or an area of publicly funded service such as education or phases of education. The discourse must of necessity become non-specialist in order to be shared and understood by the media, the general public and politicians, although, at times, the detailed professional lives of teachers and the everyday worlds of children seem to be swept up and reduced to simple headlines rather than deconstructed. Levels of accountability must also, it seems, be introduced by central office, imposed and cascaded, and such measures of effectiveness need also to be simple and easily measurable. Teaching and learning as an activity, however, do not fit neatly into pre-formed moulds or packages. Where people are concerned, rather than products, finance, industry or commerce, there are also additional levels of unpredictability, spontaneity, unique response, innovation, subversion and interpersonal challenge. In any teaching and learning encounter, human factors matter; for example, who the teacher and learner are, what prior experiences they have in common, any shared language, any common relationships and, importantly, what understanding both have of the power relations in the teaching/learning context.

Teaching and learning may be described as relational in essence (Noddings 1992: 15), dependent on individuals' knowledge, understanding and experience, motivations and levels of engagement. This theory is in direct contrast to current political understanding and the range of political theories that now prevail. In many cases schools have become part of a 'delivery agency model of education' (Young 2006) with more attention given to pre-specified targets and curriculum goals than to children or people. Nevertheless, in spite of central government demands, some of those working with the youngest children in schools and nurseries in England have tried to define an alternative pedagogy, not technicist but human, not delivery but engagement.

Young children deserve and often demand a specialised pedagogy. With brains doubling in size during the first two years of life, with 'synaptic connections' strengthening or 'atrophying' through experience or lack of it as they grow (Greenfield 2000: 61), with young children's energy and enthusiasm for conversation, experience and collaborations, their teachers' responsibility is to be relentlessly responsive, intersubjective and interactive. This way of working is supported by developmental psychologists (Vygotsky 1978; Rogoff 1990), sociologists and socio-cultural theorists (Furlong 2000; Apple 2004; Ball 2004; Pollard 2004; Hartley 2006; Young 2006) and psychology and neuro-science (Gopnik *et al*. 1999; Greenfield 2000; Immordino-Yang and Damasio 2007). By closely engaging with children as they play, teachers are able to lead by following (Rogoff 1990). Trevarthan in his (1998) work focusing on intersubjectivity has documented how, from infancy, it is often the child who initiates action and the parents or carers who join in. In playful pedagogies in educational institutions like school or nurseries, teachers are able to create contexts to enable them to follow children into play, co-constructing the action, possibly a narrative and resources. In this way it is possible to see the potential for 'the effort to communicate draw[ing] the child into a more mature understanding that is linked to what the child already knows' (Rogoff 1990: 73). In her argument for cognitive development through interaction, Rogoff also claims that 'individuals must become aware of and interested in exploring alternatives to their own perspective, and there must be intersubjectivity between partners to explore the existence and value of the alternatives' (ibid.: 142). This presupposes that teachers are able to forego preordained curricular objectives in order to pursue children's play objectives but also, and most significantly, that teachers are able to trust that cognitive development will occur in these kinds of play contexts and playful interactions without contrivance, hijacking or subverting children's intentions. Trust is a thread that occurs in the conversations of the two teachers later; trust in children as well as in their knowledge of development and learning and the contexts that they have defined as appropriate.

Those teaching professionals who are able to engage in such a playful pedagogy are now rare. They may be those, as Claxton claims (2000) who are 'willing to enter a state of confusion', who possess the skill of 'catching the inner gleam' of children (ibid.: 49) and who are able to trust both children and their own intuitive responses which, as Furlong writes, prioritises 'ways of knowing' rather than conventionally defined 'knowledge' (Furlong 2000: 28). There are such teachers who, in spite of the dominant pedagogical demands of the moment, are involved in a playful pedagogy. It is certainly evident that ascribing value to and deconstructing teachers' intuitive playfulness, in order to make the pedagogy explicit and to give it status, are always a challenge as those involved often fail to see value in that which is intuitive rather than pre-determined, and of course such practice does not sit neatly in audits or simple measures of accountability. If learning occurs in a social context (Rogoff 1990), then it is dependent upon relationships, reciprocity and language. Power structures are such that the shape of those relationships, the potential for reciprocal events and the nature of language employed are all within the control of one individual, the teacher, however strong prescriptive pedagogies may be.

There is a further concern in relation to young children's learning potential in play to consider. In Bernstein's (1977) notion of invisible pedagogies he refers to privileging texts and the transmission of dominant cultural and social principles. A clear definition of 'invisible pedagogy' is given by Hartley (1993) in his attempts to understand connections between constructs of childhood, society and pedagogy. He defines invisible pedagogy as the way in which

> control will be achieved implicitly: that is the child may rearrange and personalise the context which has been pre-defined by the teacher; the child will have the apparent discretion as to what, when, with whom and how he acts within this pre-set arrangement.
>
> (ibid.: 26)

This is, indeed, the view often to be seen in many early years settings. In such settings there will be evidence of 'apparent freedom' (ibid.: 145) although creative or strategic compliance will require such freedoms to be consigned to corners of the curriculum or the classroom. Perhaps a second layer to the concern about 'invisible pedagogies' is that they may themselves become 'visible' (Dahlberg 2000: 182) and thus they too will then become embedded in an objectives-driven curriculum. In his study across nations and cultures, while Alexander found evidence of 'oral pedagogies' (2000: 461), he predominantly describes a 'regulatory context of classroom discourse' with a 'combination of register, code and communicative management' (ibid.: 521), indicating that this combination, of rhetoric and practice, of visible and invisible pedagogies, exists more widely than may be supposed.

Hartley made a prediction that more than a decade ago may have sounded visionary, although now his claims, binding together his knowledge of education traditions and politics, and pursuing a policy trajectory, make perfect sense: 'If tradition is followed we can expect [the] policy initiatives to be couched in democratic-sounding terminology, replete with references to the needs of the individual. The discourse of developmental psychology and individualism will fuse together' (Hartley: 1993: 148). The language of current New Labour documents, with their references to 'personalised learning' may be said to coincide with Hartley's views (DCSF 2005). As Alexander reminds us, 'Pedagogy manifests the values and demands of nations, community and school as well as classrooms' (2000: 563). What then of the individuals within? It seems we have conflicting views of teacher/educators as either one-dimensional transmitters of culture and culturally defined knowledge or as 'reflective practitioner, researcher, co-constructor of knowledge, culture and identity' (Moss and Petrie 2002: 137), a complex role requiring a more radical reconstruction of popular conceptions of teaching and learning than simply adapting the vocabulary used in government documents. The question of whose purposes are being served by existing emphases in educational institutions (BERA SIG 2003: 16) is an important one and needs to be addressed at every level. Making explicit these perspectives will uncover real educational aims and intentions and make visible, at one level, upon whose values early education is built and so, too, the intended role of teachers defined within these perspectives.

Respect for children's rights and an understanding that they will also have a perspective are paramount in any discussion of 'stakeholders', a term borrowed of course from practices outside of education. It could also be argued that children themselves are the primary stakeholders in debates about education and the only stakeholders with whom teachers should be concerned. But, equally and often overlooked, is the notion that 'only children themselves can "make sense", understand and learn', no matter how much rhetoric exists in and around the domain of education (Pollard 2004: 294). It is children's control over their constructs that will ultimately make a difference to what is learned. In their review of an innovative Early Childhood, Care and Development programme with First Nation Communities in Canada, Pence and Ball locate key principles of 'respect and voice' within a 'caring, supportive and inclusive educational environment' (2000: 40) and these could also be seen as universally significant guiding principles for practice with all children and within cultures within nations.

Space for playful pedagogies

The environment or play space, which is designed and defined for young children's development and learning, reflects broad educational ideologies including that of society in general at a particular moment in history and, more specifically, that of the designers as well as the teacher who is using and controlling the space. How we conceive of education is reflected in the space we define within which practice will occur. For example, if we understand education as a way of shaping future citizens, transmitting existing knowledge, developing future adults, as Durkheim (1956) argued, then a particular built environment will serve these purposes. Educational settings would be created as closed spaces for predetermined, objectives-led practice. They would be similar in layout and content and familiar to each generation that encounters them. The alternative is to provide spaces and places for children to experience their childhood rather than to serve a curriculum; settings where children can shape and construct their own worlds and develop a sense of self as a creator, managing and controlling the space themselves, rather than being controlled by the environment. The first conception would prepare children for worlds already known, the second would encourage and nourish new possibilities and potentials and new ways of thinking and working. In Reggio Emilia pre-schools, such settings have already been created as spaces demonstrating respect for children who learn actively and who are in dialogue with others, 'active, engaged, exploring young spirits' (Gardner 2004: 17).

How educators use space, how and where teachers locate themselves, issues of power and control of and in the space, the resources and ways that interactions with resources and others take place are, potentially, all managed by individual teachers themselves. In one research project it became evident that, in spite of identical physical provision, different teachers remained rigidly within their own preferred teaching approach (McGregor 2004: 15). And so, although society may feel comfortable in physically changing the appearance and content of educational spaces, without fundamental changes in pedagogical approaches, little effective difference may be observable.

Bourdieu's notion of a 'game' of education that he claims 'everyone plays but different structures ensure that not everyone is equal' (Grenfell and James 1998: 25), suggests that it would be naïve to hope that even in defined play contexts for young children, this inequality would not be evident, either in the already established learner identity of young children, the relationship of teacher to learner or the powerful notion of selfhood.

> Social reality exists, so to speak, twice, in things and in minds, in fields and in habitus, outside and inside agents. And when habitus encounters a social world of which it is the product, it finds itself 'as a fish in water', it does not feel the weight of the water and takes the world about itself for granted.
>
> (Bourdieu 1989, cited in Grenfell and James 1998: 14)

Indeed, this may be the worrying state of current policy-making as middle-class policy-makers and politicians attempt to recreate their own schooling

(Anning 1994: 17) and middle-class educators forget to, and are discouraged from, critically appraising curriculum initiatives and centrally devised prescriptive documents. It is indeed crucial that we all feel the weight of the water in order to account for the educational worlds we create for children.

Is it in any way possible, with the weight of social structures, education policy and societal expectations, for teachers to mediate knowledge and understanding in play narratives, without the danger of children 'being crushed, diminished, converted into spectator(s), manoeuvred by myths which powerful social forces have created' (Freire 1976: 6)? Freire also claims that 'just as there is no such thing as an isolated human being there is also no such thing as isolated thinking' (ibid.: 134). Perhaps there is hope that, since teachers in the early years spend many hours a day in classrooms with young children, they will become susceptible to their collaborative needs and be sufficiently seduced by children's desires to problematise and construct meaning in their play narratives to co-join with them in their endeavours.

Chapter 4

The significance of talk

There is more to explore in order to understand the nature of storying in play and that is the essence of the engagement itself, the type of talk and in particular, the status that it is afforded in contemporary schooling. This review of the landscape of research literature began by looking at a particular aspect of institutional engagement – storying – attempts to understand the people who design and value such episodes – intuitive and playful practitioners – and ends by reviewing research into talk itself and the nature of, and elements contained within, dialogic exchange.

The notion that talk is 'a good thing' is slippery and needs to be deconstructed and properly understood. From nurseries to training institutions, talk as a tool for learning is discussed and celebrated. However, there is a continuum of practice ranging from very structured questions and answers, through Mercer's rule-governed talk (2000) towards the idea that teachers should engage in a pedagogy of listening (Rinaldi 2005) and where child-led conversations are fore-grounded and given status. Talk is celebrated today as being fundamental to the way that children think and learn. Babies and children realise early on that what they say, that is the noises they make as well as what they do, can change the behaviour of others and affect the context and the environment in which they live (Woodhead *et al.* 1998; Gopnik *et al.* 1999). Children's early language and literacy learning are bound by the models and practices they encounter, enabling them to construct meaning from experience, make inferences and shape their intentions (Rogoff 1990; Cole 1998). Even very young children have already learned to navigate their way through multiple social worlds (Dunn 1998). Indeed, 'as far as the brain is concerned, stimulation is provided by conversations, experiences and encounters' (Greenfield 2000: 63). Yet there is more to understand about the connection between talk and learning. Both Piaget's (1959) and Vygotsky's (1986) work on thought and language are helpful here.

Piaget constructed eight 'fundamental categories of speech' in his seminal work on children's language and thought and he divided these into two categories 'egocentric speech' and 'socialised speech' (1959: 9–11). It is particularly important to understand Piaget's research as it has often been misrepresented and the term 'egocentricism' needs to be rather more care-fully considered than is often the case in contemporary reviews. Piaget's claim was that children moved from an egocentric speech to socialised speech, which he believed was of a higher order. Both of these, however – that is, egocentric speech and socialised speech – are merely headlines and there are sub-divisions and subtleties contained within each category. Piaget explained them in these ways as follows.

Egocentric speech

1   repetition of words and syllables (the pleasure of talking);
2   monologue (as though he were thinking aloud);
3   dual or collective monologue (involving an outsider connected with the action but is expected neither to attend nor to understand).

Socialised speech

4   adapted information (exchange thoughts, interchange of ideas, in pursuit of a common aim);
5   criticism (affective remarks asserting superiority of the self and deprecation of others, often giving way to argument);
6   commands, requests and threats (clear interactions between children);
7   questions (those that require answers);
8   answers (to real questions and to commands).

(Piaget 1959: 10)

In play, children can be observed to engage in both pure and collective mono-logue, which Piaget describes as serving to 'accompany, reinforce or to supple-ment' children's actions (ibid.: 17). Piaget believed that children progressed through stages from egocentric speech to socialised speech and that the role of the adult is to reduce the child's soliloquy or monologue and to develop dia-logue (ibid.: 259). Indeed, he describes monologue as a 'primitive and infantile function of language' (ibid.: 17). In this study, however, the story monologues of children are given rather more status as sophisticated narrations of play, drawing on a range of cultural influences, learned behaviours and lived experiences.

Piaget's categories of speech are helpful in describing characteristics of chil-dren's language in the early years. He acknowledges the complexity involved in attempting to understand the connections between thought and language, celebrating the notion that others are engaged in such studies, and resists any attempt to reduce the functions of language to simply that of commu-nicating thought. Vygotsky (1986) extends this thinking through his research into the connection between thought and language and challenges Piaget's earlier work. Vygotsky's research demonstrates, first, that 'things', that is the 'reality that a child encounters in his practical activity ... shapes his mind' (ibid.: 40) and, second, the idea that gestures and talk serve a mediatory role in the process of concept formation. Vygotsky describes a stage 'when speech begins to serve intellect and thoughts begin to be spoken' (ibid.: 82).

Initially, he claims that:

Thought is non-verbal
Speech becomes rational.
Speech is non intellectual
Thought becomes verbal.

And that 'the speech structures mastered by the child become the basic structures of his thinking' (ibid.: 94). This notion radiates importance in terms of the conversation, experiences and encounters that neuro-science is now finding significant in relation to children's leaning and our cultural understanding that babies need conversation (Gopnik *et al.* 1999; Greenfield 2000).

Both Piaget's analysis of language (1959) and Vygotsky's (1978, 1986) research into the interconnectedness, 'interfunctional' nature, of thought and language – that the child's 'thought development is determined by language' (1986: 94) – are enormously helpful in understanding why and how children narrate their play and of course, its significance in learning and development. These rather complex ideas of how eventually we develop inner speech and learn to control our mental processes, indicate the absolute requirement for young children to engage in freely developing play contexts. Equally, the seminal research work of Piaget and Vygotsky describes the fundamental role that adults play in this process. In a passage that is perhaps ahead of its time, Piaget discusses how a child may be supported to progress through some of the categories of talk he defines and the rather delicate balance between intervention and independence:

> If the adult makes a rule of keeping to the indispensable *minimum* of interference, the child, in his intercourse with him, will fluctuate between soliloquy and interrogation, interspersed, no doubt with a small amount of embryonic discussion. But if the adult constantly intervenes, it will be up to him to reduce the child's soliloquy to a satisfactory proportion and to develop dialogue. The resulting discussions will be fundamental so far as number goes. But will their quality be comparable with that of spontaneous discussions prompted by the child's own needs? This raises all the questions relating to 'active' education and education based on authority.
> (Piaget 1959: 259)

While Piaget's work is focused upon the nature of individual children's development through talk, Vygotsky describes how, through talk, the 'nature of development itself changes, from biological to sociohistorical' (Vygotsky 1986: 99) or socio-cultural and how the presence of another, an adult, is particularly significant in effecting development. In particular, Vygotsky claims that a 'moment of mutual understanding [between child and adult] plays a decisive role in turning words into concepts' (ibid.: 123). This is the foundation of the development of inner speech.

Talking to, talking with ...

When children arrive at school, their development, including their literacy development, is already being shaped by home talk, media and peer cultures, as previously discussed (Wells 1986; Wood 1988; Whitehead 2004). Defining the role of significant adults in this process is important, that is, those who witness or co-join with children to construct talk events. The seminal work of Wells in the Bristol study (1986), which I believe to be still fundamental to all education studies, confirmed how content relevance, the child in the role of expert and being provided with the support of a listener who was interested in what the child was saying, all contributed to enhanced competence. Of course, in order for this to occur, the listener has either to be expert themselves in this level of child development theories, or respond naturally to children, as people, in a courteous manner, or behave intuitively in the company of children which would encompass both previous statements, 'braided' together (Claxton 2000).

Essential to this kind of work with children is the ability and willingness of adults to identify and respect the intentions of children. The extensive studies of those researching the impact of authentic play contexts in early education settings (see, for example, the observational studies of Hall 1987, 1999; Hall and Robinson 1995) help us to understand the significance of the play event as a vehicle for literacy learning and development. The work of developmental psychologists, however, determines the worth of the adult's presence in and around such events (Bruner 1986; Vygotsky 1986). Rogoff's work on 'guided participation' (1990) has been particularly significant as it gathers together the influence of previous work on cognitive development, taking a socio-cultural perspective on adults' roles in children's learning. Rogoff describes guided participation as 'building bridges between what children know and new information to be learned, structuring and supporting children's efforts, and transferring to children the responsibility for managing problem solving' (ibid.: viii). Her emphasis on 'interdependence' and the social nature of much of children's learning challenges previous assumptions that individual children make sense of their lives in solitary endeavours and reinforces the work of Vygotsky and others that learning occurs on two planes.

The term 'scaffolding' has been used extensively and authoritatively in writings, research and teacher education materials in recent years and, yet, it is fraught with difficulties (see vignette from Matthews, cited earlier for an example of adult 'scaffolding' as supportive nudging). As Meek (in private conversation) has pointed out, scaffolding across the world takes on different forms and is not consistently represented by an upright fixed metal structure –

in China, it may be of bamboo construction, in Greece, its wooden form ranges across the space and climbs at differing points and angles. The idea that a supporting structure could be flexible and multi-centred with the potential for differently sited high points is significant in this argument. More recently, Daniels has critiqued the scaffolding metaphor, claiming that 'it runs the risk of being appropriated and transformed by almost any set of pedagogic and/or psychological assumptions' (2007: 323). The most troublesome aspect is that it is used to reinforce the notion that there is a predetermined and fixed set of adult intentions that the child must be supported to achieve, 'the adult's intended goal' (ibid.: 322). Daniels also expresses concern that it is adults who are often defined as the scaffolders, ignoring the effect of peers in co-constructions. The claim that it is intersubjectivity that is the key to successful interactions is of supreme importance in understanding the role of adults in talk events (ibid.: 323) and the roles that some teachers assign themselves.

Communicative acts are rather more complex than may be often understood and such understanding is paramount in making sense of teacher/child interactions in play. The over-simplistic model, that a signal is transmitted by a 'sender' and received by a 'receiver', assumes 'that the sender encodes, or packages, a single meaning and transmits it to the receiver, who passively decodes or fails to decode it. The "it" remains the same throughout' (Wertsch 1991: 73). Within this model is the assumption that words are impersonal and can be decontextualised and depersonalised. However, the work of Wertsch, in his dissemination of Bakhtin's writings on dialogic enquiry, supports the idea that 'meaning' is generated as a process and that words exist in chains of other words, as 'interanimation' (ibid.: 75). In Bakhtin's own words, the complexity of speech events is laid out:

> Any concrete discourse (utterance) finds the object at which it was directed already as it were overlain with qualifications, open to dispute, charged with value, already enveloped in an obscuring mist – or, on the contrary, by the 'light' of alien words that have already been spoken about it. It is entangled, shot through with shared thoughts, points of view, alien value judgements and accents. The word, directed towards its subject, enters a dialogically agitated and tension-filled environment of alien words, value judgements and accents, weaves in and out of complex interrelationships, merges with some, recoils from others, intersects with yet a third group; and all this may crucially shape discourse, may leave a trace in all its semantic layers, may complicate its expression and influence its entire stylistic profile.
>
> (Bakhtin 1981: 276)

With this level of complexity in mind, listening to children becomes a rather different task than simply recording the oral transmission of messages. Further, Wertsch claims that 'the person-acting-with-mediational-means', that is the 'agent' in the interaction, should not fragment the action from the person or the 'mediational means' (the sign system, for example, spoken language) as 'it could mislead' (1991: 119). This claim makes very clear that the subject, the content, of the communication cannot be separated from the person communicating, or from the way in which it had been communicated. I think the idea of teachers, or adults, as knowledgeable 'insiders' is useful here, knowledgeable in socio-cultural terms, because, as Shotter claims, 'one's mind is not just a general purpose organ of general-go-anywhere-anytime intelligence, but is "at home" only in one's own times; one thinks both "out of" and "into" a certain cultural "background"' (Shotter 1993: 5). The 'mind' in question here could be construed as both the teacher's and the child's as we foray back and forth across cultures and cultural divides, in the best practice. And the cultural background could be construed as the shared play space or the shared understanding of lived lives in the homes, communities and cultures beyond the immediate place of action.

The notion of 'mutuality' is useful here too. The term has been used by Vygotsky as he describes how a 'moment of mutual understanding plays a decisive role in turning words into concepts' (1986: 123). This kind of approach, however, presupposes a special kind of adult in the relationship, one who can 'become aware of and interested in exploring alternatives to their own perspective, and there must be intersubjectivity between partners to explore the existence and value of the alternatives' (Rogoff 1990: 142). In her discussion of shared thinking and guided participation and their value in cognitive development, Rogoff establishes the view that this does not mean 'progress towards a universal goal' (ibid.: 190) but rather the participants are seeking new knowledge together, a creative process whereby 'a product is jointly produced and individually appropriated' (ibid.: 196). Such 'appropriation' is transformative, that is, it will not remain in its jointly produced state but will be transformed to map into other existing understandings and thought that are culturally owned and managed. Rogoff maintains that the 'achievement of intersubjectivity' requires those involved to 'stretch' towards a mutuality. In play, it may be the adults whose 'stretching' should be most visible.

Finally, in this discussion of talk, 'teacher talk' – the nature of the discourse in which teachers engage and work – should be further considered. The issue here to consider is that the new discourse, that of performativity and standards referred to in an earlier section, may overlay and even subsume the kind of mutuality of engagement described above. Teachers' performances, which 'serve as measures of productivity, or output ... or represent the worth, quality or value of an individual' (Ball 2004: 143) are observed and judged. The reality is that this discourse may become an 'obscuring mist' (Bakhtin 1981) masking the potential for substantial engagement in speech events in play. If, as Ball claims, the main aspects of performativity are 'comparison and commodification', then these completely miss the aim of education as described by research cited above.

All of this keeps the gaze in place – the 'professional' teacher, here defined by their grasp of and careful use of systems and procedures, and by the particular rewards and new identities that this delivers through a regressive, self regulation. It is in these ways that we become more capable, more efficient, more productive, more relevant; we become user-friendly; we become part of the 'knowledge economy'. We learn that we can be more than we were. There is something very seductive about being 'properly passionate' about excellence, about achieving 'peak performance'.

(Ball 2004: 148)

I have attempted to deconstruct the world and words of two interesting teachers who appear to have developed a metalanguage beyond contemporary performative speak, but whose words are themselves 'seductive' in their honest appraisal of their work with young children.

Summary

In this chapter I have ranged across a very broad landscape relating to children's learning and adults who teach, as well as indicating the very significant impact of political imperatives and current policy. Strong claims from research in the literature reviewed have been made for:

- a multiple layered narrative, asking the question 'Whose discourse pervades?' as a preface to Bakhtin's challenge of 'Who is doing the talking?';
- the power of story to support children in self-making;
- developing self-assurance and self-knowledge;
- the importance of play, that is play as boundaried by Bruce (1987). Play has particular significance in this work in the affordance it offers as a storymaking site, as well as its potential for offering intertextual opportunities to help children (and teacher/players) to interweave and narrativise experiences;
- the place for talk. Theories relating to the development of talk, developing voice, talk as a mediating tool and as a binding thread of experience have been discussed;
- consideration of the aims of education for young children;
- the role of adult educators, teachers, in children's play, schooling and education.

The breadth and the range of research in the literature relating to this study are immense and it must be acknowledged in this summary that the very briefest of consideration has been given to each of the areas in order that a sense of the size and scale of the landscape can be appreciated as well as the range of disciplines that have influence over its shape.

Chapter 5

Research connections

Digging
Between my finger and my thumb
The squat pen rests.
I'll dig with it.

(Heaney 2006: 2)

Seamus Heaney's biographical poetry is inspirational, and particularly the poem 'Digging', as he describes, with unremitting admiration and joy, his close observations of the detail of the skills employed by his father and his grandfather at work on the land. *His* work, though, is not to join them, or to follow their trail but to create a timeless record of it, as the final lines above show. Heaney watches the activity in the fields outside his window and without engaging in the physical acts creates a link between the known and the nearly known, the act of writing.

In the act of understanding the two teachers in this study, by creating a complex overlapping method for narrating the data and its analysis, there is a place for understanding my own identity as the author and architect of the work and indeed it may be important for all researchers to look at what is 'peculiarly ours' (Allport 1955: 40). My autobiographical notes here set the scene for a research study that binds together teachers, learners and personal enquiry.

Research and identity

I have been working in the field of education for more than 30 years, and for half of that time as a classroom teacher. My identity is bound up with teaching and learning encounters, with nudging and nurturing, with play, with story, with children and with learners. My teaching career, however, has been inseparable from research, that is, from personal enquiry into learning and into learners, teaching and teachers. My concern to investigate what I have initially claimed to be intuitive practice has been percolating for some time. My own initial teacher education was a four-year degree undertaken in the early 1970s with a backdrop of the Plowden Report (CACE 1967) and a mixture of concern for some of the ideals developed in the 1960s coupled with a sharp defence against new prescriptive, government-led directives. At that time too, teacher education (not training) included courses in the philosophy, sociology and psychology of education, and child-centredness was a key, undisputed focus. A geographic move from working for the Inner London Education Authority to a rural education authority in the early 1980s was also symbolic in that it coincided with the first rumblings of changes in education systems and new periods of accountability. The challenge for me, an experienced teacher, towards the end of this decade, seemed to be that of retaining the integrity of my own teacher education, early experience and personal and professional values while finding ways to satisfy new systems of accountability. The tension then was to ensure that children could remain at the centre of my interests as a teacher and that the curriculum was seen to serve their interests as learners rather than thwart them as individuals.

As an experienced teacher and Deputy Head Teacher, moving to work in Higher Education as an early years specialist, I was offered an opportunity to work at different levels, with undergraduate students, postgraduates and serving teachers. It also placed me in a reasonably unfettered position to better peel back the layers of influence on teaching and teachers in order to examine the core of practice, the often implicit, or tacit, nature of teaching and learning. This kind of deconstruction and refocusing of teaching priorities on children and their learning has been possible in the context of work with the youngest children in schools and nurseries while there was still an emphasis on their achievements rather than on their products or measurable outcomes.

However, as discussed earlier, new political interest in young learners, for potential long-term economic purposes, is continuing to render this phase more liable to scrutiny and subsequent redefinition by politicians and policy-makers. It is already possible to hear a chorus of voices clamouring for a more technical and visible pedagogy, simply measured and offering value for investment. This has been partly satisfied by the new Early Years Foundation Stage, a statutory document since 2008, in England. And so scrutinising carefully the work of two well-respected teachers (defined more carefully in Chapter 6) in a respectful yet rigorous research study, is timely.

If my teaching practice, with children and young adults, could be described as essentially relational in nature, moving between teacher/learner roles and combining the rational with a deep engagement, then so too is the research practice in this study. In her work, Noddings describes this kind of level of care as 'engrossment' (Noddings 1992: 16) which seems to be an apt term to mean deeply attentive behaviour in encounters with others. It has been important to start from a position of respect for the two teachers who have willingly participated in this work.

Designing a project which places such teachers centrally, in self-observation, narration and self-appraisal of their practice, was intuitive (see Claxton's definition on p. 42). From my knowledge of them as people, my understanding of their work and mine, I simply could not envisage another way for me to work with them in a project that had integrity, in terms of their professional lives and mine. Their voices needed to be central to the work, verbatim extracts were used to portray them and analyses were crafted around the extracted statements, claims and reflections. This does not, however, assume a blending of voices or an insensitivity between us towards surprises or new learning.

This approach could be seen, however, to be potentially closed in research terms and as a result it has required additional vigilance. I have chosen two teachers whose practice I celebrate. It could be argued that the potential outcome then could be predicted and only confirmed through conventional research means, that is through the use of interview and observation and subsequent analyses. That outcome would inevitably be that they are both good teachers, engaging in good practice, and they achieve good outcomes. And, importantly, they are nice to children. However, this work, and my two teachers, deserve greater understanding than this; they should also have the opportunity to dig deeply into their own practice, their motives and their influences.

How research work is conceived and documented is as important as the work itself. Notions of participant or non-participant researchers present teachers as objects of study, laboratory species, rather than collaborative examiners of pedagogy and development. This can be overcome, in part, by collective construction of realities. The two teachers in this study are not treated as research *objects* but as fully-fledged reflective and committed thinkers themselves. The reality of my research is, then, somewhat different to the rather bland scenario described above. The teachers were asked a series of hard questions, which led on to other hard questions – about their practice, their values, their principles, their influences and about who they think they are as teaching professionals.

'Thought' by D.H. Lawrence (1972) portrays the complexity of bringing thoughts to consciousness and these ideas relate closely to the research process. As in thought, during the process of my study, this research, all three of us were reading what could be read, pondering over experience and, importantly, wholly attending (Lawrence 1972), rather than playing a game called 'research' as some critics of this kind of research approach might believe (see, for example, critical perspectives offered in Hughes and Sharrock 1997 and Nisbet 2006).

It is true, however, to say that the relationship between researcher and researched may become almost perilously blurred at times. In asking the questions of the two participants, I was also challenging myself to justify my own teaching identity. Consequently, as they spoke, my work – as a teacher of young children, as an adult educator and as a researcher – was being examined. Is it then possible that the teachers in this study can be seen as objective appraisers of their own practice if I had, first, evaluated their work highly and, second, placed myself alongside them as similar pedagogues?

Given this self-posed question, the challenge for me has been to find a way to give validity to my analyses, to enable my voice to be heard authoritatively as the researcher's voice. I am claiming that I am an important part of the research and acknowledging both my insiderness and my agency as a writer framing or 'spinning' the research story that I am relating (Holliday 2002: 128).

Holliday's work reaches towards notions of validity for qualitative research and he claims that 'researchers must *submit* themselves to what they see and hear, by consciously and strategically being aware of and managing their own prejudices about how things are' (Holliday 2008: 1). This state of consciousness is effectively a requirement of qualitative work in that it does not deny subjectivity but instead acknowledges it as a fact and draws it into the research equation. Holliday also stresses that 'submission' allows 'realities which are beyond the initial vision of the researcher to *emerge*' (ibid.: 1).

In later chapters it will become clear that what has emerged in my study has been the very detail of two teachers' ideologies; the detail of what it is that underpins their work with children, their aims and their values. Without studying them in this depth, and I believe in this way, it would not be possible to understand their motives, influences or intentions or to understand what it is that drives and nourishes teachers to persist in practice that is not universally valued in any public or political sense.

In a sense, it has felt to me very similar to the way that one views a painting; the first response is an impression (they are good teachers), the second is a brief appraisal (they are operating in a respectful and relational way – described earlier – with children in play contexts), then the real questions (How are they achieving that?, What have they invested?, Where has it emerged from?, What do they understand about it all?). It is always possible, and sometimes desirable, to answer questions about a painting without the company and input of the artist. The discursive presence of the artist, however, lends another narrative layer to one's understanding of the art – not to supplant individual interpretation, but to colour it, to enhance and enrich it, to provide an opportunity for a joint intellectual endeavour and to provoke thought. Perhaps research of this nature should be described as synthesis as, in a similar way to the research paradigm described by Clough, in respect of children, their teachers and the researcher, it perhaps 'draws fitfully on data as well as dreams, hunches and histories, causes and cases, transcriptions and transgressions, morals and meanings' (Clough 2002: 9).

While ultimately all the research responses have been filtered through and by me into this report of the study, and in fact it may be impossible to avoid 'interposing a veil' (Nisbet 2006: 13), the very fact of this could only occur in trusting relationships between those acting in practice and those collaborating in de-mystifying and understanding such practice through informal autobiographical detail and reflexive commentary. There has been some research work on intersubjectivity and this is an area that also fits this study. Through exploring the notion that intuitive educators are those who are capable and interested in reading the intentions of others, it may be that not only in the classroom but also in the research space there is inevitably an element of social dancing.

Finally, what I have hoped to achieve in this study is an honest attempt to critically interrogate early years practice through the critical interrogation of early years practitioners, supporting them in their own interrogations of their intentions for their own work with children.

Summary

In this chapter, I have claimed that:
- autobiography and identity are inevitable ingredients of research;
- how research is conducted is significant;
- teachers' own voices deserve to be respected and heard;
- Holliday's work claiming validity for such research work requires 'submission, emergence and personal knowledge' to be acknowledged.

Part II

The Teachers' Story

Chapter 6

Narratives of practice and experience

Introduction

As discussed earlier, it is often claimed either that teachers are technicians or that 'teaching is a personal activity' (Nias 1989) and so research into professional practice is either viewed in an overly simplistic way or is shrouded in the mystery of personality. Exposing, laying bare, and examining the values, intentions and ideologies of teachers working with young children, and particularly those teachers who make claims for complexity in their practice, are necessary to help to understand the impulses that drive particular ways of working with children, specifically ways of collaborating and co-constructing in play. Evaluating practice in this way fulfils the expectation that a 'responsible professional decision depends in a large part on the quality of personal deliberation and reflection' (Carr 2000: 24). In Carr's judgement, and in his consideration of professional values and ethics, he claims that teachers need a combination of technical skills, in which he includes communication, management and organisation, with skills of evaluation to provide a context of 'professional judgement' (ibid.: 111). It is with this evaluative frame at the centre that credibility can be given to claims of professional expertise. In this chapter I will introduce both teachers, Janette and Matthew, offering some brief biographical information and will present the narratives of practice and experience that have been offered in dialogue, which serve to illustrate well these evaluative skills.

There are two teachers in this research study. They are experienced teachers. Both participants are considered to be 'successful' practitioners as evidenced by recent Ofsted inspections and the fact of their promotions. Both of the participants appear to engage in 'human encounters' in their practice (McLean 1991). This kind of 'purposive sampling' (Robson 2002: 265) was chosen because it was clear that both teachers were engaged in the kind of practice that I was interested in researching. Data have been collected from these two nursery teachers, Janette and Matthew, who are both of a similar age.

First interviews

Each of the participants was interviewed separately at the beginning of the study for two purposes: (1) to gather some simple biographical material; and (2) to develop a reflective relationship with the researcher and the research. In this sense, the first interviews set the tone and the tenor of the study by creating opportunities for the teachers to seriously consider, I think for the first time, themselves and their role as professional educators in a semi-conversational manner. As I was known to both in different roles, it was important to create a fine balance between a reasonably relaxed conversational approach and a structured research interview. To facilitate this, the first interview was not taped but recorded as field notes, while rigour was introduced by the use of a careful structure to enable responses to be as carefully and faithfully scribed as possible. A version of Kelchterman's (1993) five-part theory relating to the notion of a 'professional self' was used (Sammons *et al.* 2004) and the following questions were asked:

1   Self-image: how would you describe yourself in your profession?
2   Self-esteem: how do you evaluate yourself as a teacher?
3   Motivation: why are you committed to the job?
4   Task perception: how do you define your job?
5   Future perspectives: what are your expectations of your job?

Janette's story

Janette is 38. She is currently Teacher in Charge at a nursery, working with a large team of teachers, nursery nurses and NVQ trained staff. Although Janette studied for a National Association of Maternal and Child Welfare Diploma (NAMCW), her father encouraged her to also take A Levels and to train as a teacher. Her ITE programme focused on children from 7–11 and she graduated in 1990. Janette later took a Post-Graduate Nursery Conversion course. She has recently achieved an MA in Early Years.

Self-image

Janette found this first section rather difficult, as if she was unused to reflecting on her self and her role. She described herself as 'taking it all seriously' and 'doing it all as properly as you can, resisting the temptation to say "that will do"'. This high level of commitment became a key thread in the study and such comments began to epitomise Janette's work ethic in her nursery. The second thread that became evident at this early stage concerned relationships. Janette talked about how surprised she is at how significant she had become in parents' lives, and at how 'individual children matter'. She described her job as 'working with children and their families'. Although not working in a school context, Janette felt it important to describe herself as a teacher; she felt it raised her status.

Self-esteem

Janette described herself at a new stage, 'I'm not so jumpy about Ofsted now.' She also claimed that 'my practice is good, I work at it' but then worried that it made her sound arrogant and tried to rectify it by raising the status of her team 'when people praise us – it's not just me' and setting herself in a broad and variable context, 'I think I look good because others are not' but also assuring me that she knew where her practice could be improved.

Motivation

Reference was made to a mentor, a more senior teacher she had worked with earlier in her career: 'C taught me, we never do anything for staff convenience, if you do it, you do it properly.' Janette referred back to families, citing 'involvement and attachment' with families and communities as a key motivating factor as well as not wanting to let people down once she realised 'what you mean to people'. Another issue in this section was the need to prove that the non-school sector could be 'as good' as schools, a fact that Janette was very keen to celebrate. And finally, Janette talked about wanting to learn, 'I want to fill in the gaps, but I seem instead to open chasms!', relating to her apparent need to strive for better practice and new understandings. At this stage, Janette was in the middle of her Masters studies, reading extensively and critically appraising her own and others' practice.

Task perception

Her first response here was to immediately relay conflicts she experienced in her role, focusing initially on parents and tensions she had felt between the claims of children and of parents and how these had been competing in her mind, 'I wondered whether I was here for the child or the parents' and 'it was always the difference between what was right for parents or the child; I felt pushed towards parents'. Janette's responses were very much in the past tense at this stage, 'school felt like compensating for parents' and teaching was something that she 'did to the child in isolation – how does this mean I behaved?' This rather self-critical, judgemental stance taken by Janette became something of an underpinning theme throughout all research conversations. Her responses were made ponderously as she worried over every angle of each question; at this stage there were fewer positive reflections than self-critical and often perplexed responses. She talked of developing a more 'realistic understanding', a 'grounded understanding' as she realised that the work she did with children was 'individualised'. The focus of her responses remained with parents and families: 'if the family's struggled and continues to struggle, then what are we doing about it?'.

Future perspectives

Janette described her job here as 'plate spinning. Which are the most important plates to spin, which ones must I not let crash?' Her next response occurred after a moment or two of complete silence.

Janette said (in relation to children):

> I like them. I look. I listen. And I join in. And I wonder. I interact. And I talk. Although you don't think of it, you're looking to spin that child's plate.

She commented that 'my dad does this when he plays with us and the children'. This reference to her dad occurs again later in the study, when Janette tries to describe her relationship with children. Her apparent respect for mentors in her life and work is discussed later. Finally in this section, Janette worries about 'the dangers of losing the moment' with children in her care. It is interesting that with the single prompt of 'What are your expectations of your job?', Janette talks reflectively only of her understanding of her role and conveys the idea in this retrospection that her aspirations relate only to self-improvement rather than self-gratification in career terms.

Janette's responses indicate a thoughtful, self-critical teacher whose first priorities are to the children, families and communities with whom she works. All of Janette's teaching experience has been in, what she describes as, 'deprived, challenging areas'. Her answers are given with care and are always sensitive and often self-deprecating. She is clearly uncomfortable with any sense of self-appraisal or any potential for self-aggrandisement. She appears in this first interview to be a highly committed teacher – as committed to families as to the children, concerned to learn more and to fulfil her role as thoroughly as possible.

Matthew's story

Matthew is 36 with a first degree in history and economics. After volunteering at a local primary school he undertook a post-graduate programme in primary education and took the 3–7 course, he said 'by chance'. During this course he focused on Years 1 and 2 and received only two afternoon lectures on the Foundation Stage and Year R. He then took a temporary post in a reception class, working for a headteacher from whom, he claimed, he developed 'a feeling for what is right'. At the time of the interview Matthew had worked for seven years in the same school, all of which had been divided between nursery and reception, initially with a day a week in nursery and four days in reception and then full-time in the nursery unit.

Self-image

Matthew characterised himself as 'someone who thinks that relationships are the most important thing with parents and children – without them you have nothing'. It becomes evident throughout all conversations with Matthew that the development of relationships is at the core of his professional values. He repeats one phrase on several occasions – 'we're all in this together', referring to the notion of community, of learning communities. Throughout the seven years of Matthew's experience, he has felt it important to position himself alongside learners and talks about learning together with the children, and with parents, 'getting parents to feel they're part of the learning process. I value what they've done and are doing'. Matthew emphasises his point about relationships with the children 'I'm not putting on an act, that's not a proper relationship, I'm being myself.' In the same vein, Matthew feels that his name matters: 'There's a lot in the name; they call me Matthew; it helps the relationship, counteracts the barriers.'

Self-esteem

Matthew's evaluation of himself as a teacher is 'pretty high'. He quotes Ofsted as saying that his practice is good but claims that 'it's better than good'. He also cites feedback from parents, teachers and children as positive. In his self-evaluation Matthew comments that he has created 'a happy learning environment' where the children are independent and where there is 'so much for them to explore, investigate, grab their interest'. Matthew is clear about the complexity of his role in the nursery, saying that when he looks around and all of the children are engaged, he realises that others would not understand, would think 'that's easy'.

Motivation

Matthew had undertaken some occasional lecturing opportunities at a university. He was clear in his response that this had in part made him realise what was important about his own job. He talked about knowing whole families, mentioning relationships as important again and reiterating, for the third time, that 'we're all in it together', 'I know brothers and sisters, mum and dad too', 'you're part of the whole family'. Matthew's respect for children also became apparent, 'Children are amazing, they're amazed at what seems ordinary; it's awe and wonder with little children.'

Task perception

Matthew was unhesitating in the responses to this section which asked for a job definition. He started by firmly stating that 'Knowledge is a small part, I've just got more confident that that's not the most important part of my role.' He lists aspects of his role as 'listening, observing, talking, playing – a bit of a playmate, more of an equal' and claims that children lead and make decisions in the nursery: 'it's for them to come to me, not for me to decide what's important to them', and further 'I've not always got an agenda to move on, you've got to let them take you.' He also described how, in play and explorations, he never wanted to know what was going to happen before the children, a risky position for a teacher to take.

Future perspectives

Matthew talked here about his worries for children, his concern about 'stages and ages' and his dismay about children 'failing' in these early stages. He described his role as partly 'consultation' and that he watched what children actually did in classroom areas and thought about how he could make these spaces more interesting. He said that he 'never feels like I'm just plodding along. I'm always thinking about what's working and how children are responding and so on.' In this section, Matthew talked about gender issues, that it was good for the children to see a man around the place, but also his view that men are different with children, do risky things, 'things that make people go ooooh'. He said that he tried to do something 'edgy' every day, that 'male teachers are not so precious about things' and that sometimes 'it can get a bit lovely' in early years practice. These views are reminiscent of Bronfenbrenner's claims for additional adults, other members of the family or from the outside world to be involved in support for, in particular, the mother–child dyad and his recommendation that the balance of power is such in settings that children feel able to innovate (Bronfenbrenner 1979).

Matthew's responses were reflective and generally assured. His commitment to the children and their families shone out of his reflections and his passion for engaging children in their nursery world was also very evident. He made very strong references to relationships, emphasising that these must be authentic between people, and created the image of a teacher concerned to create a community of learners that included parents and families. He felt that the 'teacher thing', the status of teacher, could be a barrier to learning in this context with young children and claimed that the use of his first name, his approach to creating equality as far as possible in play and in his relationships with the children, all contributed to the children's trust in him.

The teachers in this study, rather than allowing themselves to become technicians are engaged in 'teaching as a personal activity' (Nias 1989). In his consideration of professional values and ethics, Carr claims that teachers need a combination of technical skills, in which he includes communication, management and organisation, with skills of evaluation to provide a context of 'professional judgement' (Carr 2000: 111). Making sense of this idea of professional judgement in early years education will contribute to the development of a theory of practice, not for prescriptive purposes but for the more important reason of exemplification to form a hypothesis about intuitive teachers and teaching and about the nature of their affective encounters with children.

First observation

Both of the teachers were observed during a normal session, in as unobtrusive a manner as possible. Although I was introduced to the group in both settings, the children took little or no notice of me, except as occasionally an extra pair of hands to do up a button or untie a ribbon.

Observing Janette: I

In Janette's nursery the children arrive and go with their parents or carers directly to their assigned group leaders who are situated at designated places around the nursery room. The children are greeted informally, coats hung up and parents and children exchange news, information, pictures, etc. or the children go directly to an activity, resource or to an area of their choice. Some children go directly to the snack area. Janette herself is available then to individually greet parents or carers, to receive information or to be consulted. Following this, most parents leave, although some stay for portions of the session for various reasons. During the children's play, Janette moved between groups, sometimes systematically trailing key children, sometimes more broadly observing and sometimes engaging fully in play scenarios. She initially moved into the room with a child who had just arrived and was looking at the fish tank. The following extract has become very significant to me in exemplifying the complexity of engagement in informal contexts with children and the nature of spontaneous storying:

J: We've got hamster babies.
Child 1:   Me got hamster babies.
J: Lots of hamster babies – it's like the whole world's full of hamsters.
J: I wonder if fish like yoghurt.
Child 1:   Well, they'd need a spoon.
Child 2:   I've put a mermaid in the cupboard.
J: Is it a dolly?
Child 2:   No, it's a mermaid.

In order to understand this rather surreal extract of a single moment of informal conversation, it is important to appreciate the readiness of all concerned, adults in this nursery context and children, to move between versions of reality and imaginary worlds. Equally important, however, is the need to appreciate the complex nature of these kinds of encounters and how possible it is to make mistakes or to tread in exactly the wrong space, for example, Child 1's real-world response about a fish needing a spoon to eat yoghurt and Child 2's correction about the doll existing in an imaginary world as a mermaid. This exchange, however, took only a few moments before the children entered into other activities with other children and other resources, apparently content that they had imparted important information, or at least said what they wanted to say. In Janette's work, these kinds of encounters were frequent.

At this point Janette climbed up the ladder of the wooden play structure to the play house level where a group of four girls were playing with dolls and play house food, sandwiches, pizza and bread. She says:

J: Hello, is that your baby? She wants some toast, she whispered in my ear.
    Have you got any strawberry jam?
    There is some toast but no strawberry jam to put on it.
    The dinosaurs might like to eat the toast.
    Do you know, I think you've had burglars in your house! It's in a terrible mess.
    Look at S's house [another play house on the other side of the room where they move to for the next section of play] – she's got a lot of tidying up to do.
    Yummy, yummy, mmm, beans and sausages.
    Where's the knife gone – that's a spoon?
    Can you believe it? They've left all this food on the floor.
    (Janette begins to pick up from the floor and the other children join in with her.)

Janette's talk is often a narration of the action of play as it is played, providing a vocabulary, sometimes extending ideas, modelling behaviour and questioning while at the same time physically participating. Rogoff describes this as the way in which 'middle-class adults often search for common reference points, translating the adult understanding of the situation into a form that is within children's grasp' (Rogoff 1990: 72). Unconsciously, Janette is initially, herself, constructing understandings of the moment, shaping them to make them intelligible to children and overlaying them onto the children's actions, thereby, implicitly shaping their view of the world, drawing them into her assumptions of shared understanding.

However, one of her intentions for this episode of play participation became apparent in the next narrative extract. Janette says:

J: Look, Bj's going to make food for her baby.
I think they want their dinner before they go in their cot.
Where can that baby sit? Have you got space in that one?
Are you making all the beds? Is that a potty there – we don't want a potty in the bed. (laughing)
Look, L's sorting all the dollies out.
Can Bj come as well – over here?
Are we all having a sleep? Is it a sleepover place?
Where shall we sleep? On the pillow?
I can unstrap him – is he going to bed too?
I hope his tummy doesn't grumble all night.
It's too late for supper – oh, a midnight feast.
Make a space for our supper in bed.
We need a blanket for our legs.
You've got a load of stuff there – what have we got?
Ooh, what's on there? More supper?
Has he had any?

...

Oh, I've got to ssh – it's sleep time now.

...

You want to sleep too, K? Is there room?
Ask them to squeeze up.

In this clutch of narrative, lasting just a moment or two while she climbs into bed under a blanket with a small group of children, Janette works hard at ensuring inclusion. Her pronouns move effortlessly from 'he' and 'you' to 'we' and 'our' and her intention to include the particular child Bj into this group of girls' play appears to be successfully and unobtrusively achieved. At the same time, lessons related to sharing and making space are embedded in her ongoing relation of events. At all times Janette appears to be led rather than leading, to be questioning rather than instructing and content for the children to direct the play forward. Her language, vocabulary choices, of 'sleep-over', 'supper', 'midnight feast' undoubtedly reflect her own childhood influences (Blyton perhaps), her own experiences as well as her own parenting understanding, about which more will be said. This session ended naturally as children giggled and fell out of bed or moved on and Janette noticed another child in need of attention and moved herself to another story space in the nursery. As she did so, Janette wrote her observation notes quickly on a Post-it sticker pad. A very brief conversation was held between us, as the session was still in progress, and Janette was keen to celebrate individual children and reiterate some of the goals and achievements of the children during the session

Observing Matthew: I

Matthew had gathered the children into the nursery carpet corner after an initial free flow play session. Some of the children were in dressing up clothes. His purpose was to choose the prince and princess for the afternoon and to formally crown them on their thrones. Abigail was chosen as princess for the afternoon because she 'knew where things were and where to put away'. Matthew told the children that this was called being independent, doing things by herself. Arty was chosen to be prince because he had 'found so many different ways of making sounds [a current topic]; even if he had the same thing he made different sounds with it'. Arty called out 'I did, I did loads of things' and Matthew replied 'You did, and that's why you're the prince!' In this small vignette, Matthew was indicating to the children those attributes and attitudes that he valued and would reward, not necessarily those of the most able, competent or adept child. He did so in a quietly, understated but effective manner, drawing the whole group with him so that they were able to recognise and praise the children who were crowned for their achievements. Following this, the children were invited to plan to play. They were all invited to hold on to each other, behind Matthew who took them on 'the planning train' in Highscope style, chugging around the nursery, whistling to a halt at every resourced area for children to get off if they so wished. During this play session, snacks were available to the children at a designated table and the children were aware that they could choose to sit and snack if they wanted to.

By the end of the train ride only Billy was left on 'the train' which had come to a halt by the large block area. At this point, as Billy hovered near the bricks, Matthew decided to take the blocks out onto the outside play area. Billy helped, another child ran to join them. The children spent 20 minutes building a rocket, running back and forth to get the blocks and some milk crates for seats. During this period Matthew's verbal contributions were often barely audible and they complemented, rather than narrated, action. For example, Matthew made only 17 utterances in the 20-minute observed play period and they were all similarly unobtrusive as these examples show:

Matthew: I think Sam might be blasting off here.
Tell me what it's going to be, Billy?
Is it part of the rocket?
Have you got a place to sit on your rocket?
Is there room for 2?
Are you going to hop on board then?
Right, Sam's in place, Billy.
Are you off, you're off.
Press the blast off button.

Billy: It's taking me to school.
Matthew: Wish I had a rocket to go to school, Billy – a good way to travel.
            Would you take your mummy on the rocket?

He asked questions without always having the expectation of them necessarily being answered and always placing the children in the role of expert. Rogoff's claim (1990: 18) that in middle-class homes 'social interaction and children's activities are not designed explicitly for the future edification of the children' seems also to apply to Matthew's practice. Rogoff continues:

> Most of children's lives involve interactions and social arrangements that are organized to accomplish the task of the moment and may carry tacit lessons for alert children, without being explicitly or intentionally focused on communication or instruction.
>
> (ibid.: 18)

This play interaction involved no instructional talk at all. Instead it involved Matthew in helping children to accomplish their 'task of the moment', which was to build a rocket and there were tacit lessons for the children. For example, he referred constantly to Billy as the instigator of the project thereby giving him the status that was evidently needed. At the same time, he ensured the other child, and later other children, were included without any need for assertion with his 'is there room for 2?' question. Although mention of the moon as the destination had been made earlier, Matthew completely accepted Billy's decision that the rocket would be going to school, without negative comment, continually modelling responses for the benefit of all of the children.

Matthew's physical presence was close to the children but not inside their play and construction zone. He was used to fetch and carry blocks, was accepted but not deferred to. The children were the decision-makers at all times. As the 20 minutes ended and the session's end drew near, I noticed that Matthew took an opportunity to write his observations quickly on his sticker pad.

Comment

This first observation created the first surprise of the study. Although both teachers were known to me, through contact on other research projects and work with students as well as previous visits to both settings, for the purposes of this research, observations through a different lens and analysis were required. During the process of reviewing the observations and analysing the data, I realised that, actually, the practice of the teachers was considerably different even though I had assumed, most recently from the interview data, that they would be working in similar, if not the same ways. There were clear similarities:

- Both demonstrate absolute respect for children, their families and the community context in which their schools were situated.
- Both demonstrate absolute respect for play, play stories and play contexts.
- In both practices, the power of their relationships with the children is evident.
- In both practices, knowledge of the children is implicit in talk and actions.
- Both teachers appear to be intuitive in their responses and their practice generally.
- There was evidence of complete trust in the teachers by the children.
- There was no apparent predetermined 'direction' to the play.

The differences, however, were highly significant:

- Janette initiates, models, participates, multi-voices, is a player.
- Matthew is an 'addressee', leaves respectful spaces, observes more than plays.
- The pace of interactions in each nursery is significantly different.

Janette took more of a focal role in the play, narrating the play activities and therefore sometimes initiating acts and modelling play behaviours while in role with the children. She used a range of voices during play, including that of player, leader, helper, model, shaper, listener, responder, all of which, and more, might be said to constitute the role of 'teacher'. Her narrations kept pace with the flow of the play actions.

Matthew was often a silent observer/player, appearing useful to the children for carrying or helping to construct but often a lesser player rather than a lead. The way that Matthew behaves can be described as 'addressivity' and this is important in the context of play dialogues. Carter uses Bakhtin's work to explain this idea: 'Addressivity underlines the importance of an addressee, a listener who can also have a creative role to play in a dialogue, even if sometimes only a silent, non-verbal one' (Carter 2004: 68).

Matthew's responses were intermittent and relaxed. He was quite often silent. His delivery of response was reflective and measured and this all invariably impacted on the pace of play and the status of such reflective moments during the play.

When discussing these behaviours with the teachers following the observations, they commented that, when playing with the children 'you best guess their intentions and purposes', 'observing, listening and making sense of what you see', 'influencing but not imposing'. They talked about how these pedagogical decisions were made and about influences that shaped their practice: 'Everything I do now comes from me, at the core, and experiences, courses, children and colleagues', 'significant others', 'Subconsciously, these influences get caught, like a filter, some things stick', 'It's about being professional.' There seems to be a sense in this conversation that the teachers are describing a 'melding' of who they believe they are with what they have experienced and how they viewed their professional roles; all intrinsically concerned with teacher identity.

Research conversations

I had now interviewed both teachers separately, observed them in their practice and had a brief and informal conversation with them following the observation. The teachers then met together with me to revisit what had been discussed so far, to watch each other's video material and to continue the discussion about what was causing them to teach in the way that they were teaching. The question of 'What do the teachers believe they are doing?' had in many different ways already been considered, in particular during the first interviews. I now needed to further pursue this so that they could articulate their core professional aims and to ascertain what 'being professional' actually meant to them. Related to this is the second series of questions of 'Why do they do the things they do?, What do they hope to achieve for themselves and/or for the children?, What is their ultimate aim or short-term objectives?' I also required further elucidation in relation to the question of 'What is informing them?' and we held a discussion of these issues in relation to their knowledge of public policy and their intuitive practice. In order to facilitate this discussion, a copy of Figure 6.1 was provided for both teachers at the meeting and further explanations for these headings were also given.

Value

What practices
do I value and
most believe in?

Political

Which practices do
others most/least
approve of?

my practice

Empirical

Which practices can be
shown to be most
effective in promoting
learning?

Pragmatic

Which practices work
best (or do not work)
for me?

Conceptual

What is practice? What are
its essential elements?

Figure 6.1 Conversation prompts

While the diagram and its explanations were made available and introduced in conversation, the teachers only used it as an initial prompt rather than as an agenda for the conversation and soon moved away from it and on to pursue their own lines of thought.

Both teachers claim to be 'reluctant shapers' and yet there is subtle evidence that, as in all adult–child interactions, whether implicit or not, as Rogoff claims (1990), whether by design or not, tacit lessons may be learned by the children. And so the questions, 'In what knowing ways are they shaping the children?' and 'Is there any sense in which they feel they are manipulating the play?' both need to be answered. While the teachers were surprised that there could be any doubt about the need for, or existence of, cultural trans-missions (we discussed their simple insistence on 'please' and 'thank you', taking turns and similar standard and often embedded cultural practices), they were robust in their claims that their intentions were not to mould children's behaviours. The examples used were viewed as being intrinsically important and not in question. Equally, questioning the tidiness of the playhouse (see earlier examples) appeared to be spontaneously delivered, not particularly retained as significant, nor considered to be especially worthy of deconstruction, connecting in part to Bernstein's notion of an invisible pedagogy (Bernstein 1997).

In response to the question 'What do you think you're doing?', the teachers expressed ideas and behaviours have been observed that can be grouped under the following headings: relationships, addressivity, consensual collaboration, multi-voicing, seeking mutuality, and leading or being led. Throughout my conversations, observations of the teachers and the period of analyses, practice relating to these groupings continues to be evident. Each of these terms will be further discussed later in the study. However, progressing from this stage, a developing, and now rather central challenge in the research conversations in the second stage of this study, has been to ask the teachers 'Who do you think you are?' in order to enable some deconstruction of both role and identity and the relationship between the two. The teachers' conversation has moved in this sense from expressing some understanding of their actions towards what might be said to underpin these, their sense of themselves as teachers and their professional identity within the political and policy context described earlier.

This question, 'Who do you think you are?' has a dual function: while its first is literally to require some personal definition of identity with the stress on the question word 'who', the second purpose is to challenge the teachers' sense of autonomy and authority with the stress on the second half of the question. This test of any sense of professional authority is in answer to the kind of challenge made by Durkheim (1956) of the functional and societal requirements of education and therefore the public accountability of public servants who work in the field. Those teachers who are employing a funda-mentally 'relational' approach to their pedagogical choices are not working within the current, political imperative to frame teaching as a technical act. Such teachers, in answer to the question asked earlier by Bakhtin (Who is doing the talking?), are doing their own talking and furthermore allowing children to do their talking, thus allowing a democratic process to evolve in the early years of education. It could be said, however, that they have both a moral and a professional duty to be accountable for such practice and that their public duty needs to be achieved, although not necessarily through conventional testing arrangements.

'No one's got a clue how things should be'

Significantly, both participants in this study were very knowledgeable about current policies directly impacting on their practice as well as the broader political platform in relation to early years education now in evidence. However, their responses in relation to questions focusing upon the purposes of education centred completely on children as individuals in their care rather than the bigger policy picture, as is evidenced when they said:

> It's helping them to enjoy now, not preparing them … helping them find things they might like to explore; didn't explore as confidently as they might; take more risks … it's about helping children to be who they are; explore their strengths.
> Being with them to make sense, discovering what's going on.
> Being comfortable with who they are.
> Creating a place where they can develop decent human relationships.
> Helping children to have more control over their own lives.

The teachers were confident in responding to the prompt and equally confident in asserting their understanding of their pedagogic role, primarily in these responses as 'helpers'. The language of 'helping', 'exploring', 'creating' is evidence of a child-centred pedagogy rather than an imposed curriculum and subject-based practice. Also, in these responses, it is possible to see the ethical grounds on which the two teachers are basing their practice. This kind of ethical knowledge has been described as 'the *specialised knowledge* base of teaching expertise' (Campbell 2003: 138, author's italics), which mirrors closely one participant's view reported earlier that 'knowledge is a small part, not the most important part, of my role', in reference in this case to curriculum subject knowledge. Here a clear dichotomy is being forged between 'specialised knowledge' of the child, children's development and learning and an appropriate pedagogy centred on that knowledge and curriculum knowledge which often appears to be the central driving force of central government policies and considers children's play opportunities somewhat differently.

Language is neither separate from meaning nor from the meanings and values held by the person making use of it, and so 'there is no such thing as a "general language", a language that is spoken by a general voice' (Holquist, 1981: xxi). As Bakhtin claims, 'the word does not exist in a neutral and impersonal language (it is not, after all, out of a dictionary that the speaker gets his words!)' (Bakhtin 1981: 294). It may be, however, that in the research conversations, when speaking about mutuality in play discourse, the teachers were also seeking a level of mutuality with each other and with me, as researcher. These relationships will be considered further in subsequent chapters, however, the engagement evident in the transcripts and the additional emphasis often placed on certain aspects or words used in responses indicate a very personal and very heavy investment in play interactions. During our conversations the term 'genuine' was used, as in, for example, 'I'm *genuinely* interested in why and how children are doing the things they do.' This insistence on authenticity – an honest approach – in their role as teacher has shone through as in, for example, 'If you want to get to the children, build up real relationships, it's no good being the teacher.' Of course, children can 'sense when teachers genuinely care about them; they can sniff out hypocrisy in a flash; and they are alert to differences between the supercilious and the authentic' (Campbell 2003: 23) and young children invariably act upon their knowledge – either trusting their teacher or not. Experienced teachers of young children know this. Rogoff describes children as 'tuned to pick up the interpretation and viewpoint of others' (Rogoff 1990: 73) and often active in pursuing interaction. In this study the participants frequently spoke, in Rogoff's terms, of 'inserting their interaction into the ongoing activity' and 'bridging understanding' (ibid.: 79). Although Rogoff is describing research with infants (and this age range may span 3–7 year-old children), the same is easily applied to the work of these teachers with younger children, 3- and 4-year-olds:

> What's important to me is you see what the child's intention is – you feed into it. I let it go where its going. You can do it by leading, modelling. Show them another way to play. You have an alertness to likelihoods. You respond to how she makes sense of things.

This kind of joint participation is very evident in the teachers' work with the children as they became co-players rather than instructors: guides rather than leaders. 'Tuning in' to children's play also demonstrates the value being placed on children's intentions and their ability to create the context for learning. From these comments it is evident that the teachers' role is not being viewed as passive but responsive and active, drawing on a range of professional skills such as modelling, observing, interpreting and playing. The teachers are also demonstrating confidence in the children, trusting them to learn through their play as they, the teachers, make sense of what they see, feed into the children's intentions, offer alternate ways to play and seize potential moments in play. Overall, however, the children's purposes remain paramount for these two teachers, even as they construct bridges towards new knowledge and new understandings. It is invariably the knowledge needed for the moment in play and the understandings required to facilitate the play event that seem to concern them.

Research conversations 2

On the occasion of the second meeting, the conversation was very much seen as a continuation of previous occasions, beginning with a brief précis of where we had got to and a prompt asking 'How do you know where any of it [your practice] comes from?'

Janette claimed that she left her initial teacher education feeling 'quite muddled' about what she was going to be doing in her first teaching role. Her responses focused particularly on the mentors that she encountered in her early career: 'My practice has come from a big run of very positive, very committed interactions with people.' She talked enthusiastically about the community of young teachers with whom she worked in her first post and how that extended to union activities and close relationships also with the community beyond the school. It is important to note here Janette's concern with community, from colleagues in school to colleagues in the union. With equal enthusiasm Janette described her first visit to her next school and how she 'instantly knew, ha ha, this is the place for me'. In addition, her father has been, and continues to be, a key mentor and a strong influence on her behaviour with children, her own and those in her nursery. She explains that they both talk to children in similar ways and that he is 'genuinely interested and genuinely valuing of them and treating them as a full person'. Janette explained how her father insisted that her own babies were always positioned or seated physically close to adults and treated as if they were part of the conversational context, saying that they needed to be 'part of the party'. From her father, Janette believed she had learned 'something about belonging' and 'treating children as worthy':

> I don't think about it consciously but when you try and unpick it, I suppose that's what I do, although at the time I don't think 'Oh, I must be respectful', but maybe that's where that comes from, you know, if children talk, you stop and listen just as when a grown-up talks. And if they talk over you, you try very hard to say, 'Excuse me one minute, I'll talk to you in a moment', but you do go back and say, 'What was that you were telling me?, I couldn't listen properly', rather than the kind of seen and not heard thing. And I suppose that's where that comes from, I don't know.

Matthew talked in a similar way about his mentors early in his career. When asked what influences he thought had made him the teacher that he is, Matthew replied: 'It's got to be your parents and how you grew up and your friends and family and your family relationships … something innate, a family thing.' And again, it was his first contacts in his first school that seemed to have an impact, either because he felt that they shared similar values or because he could see himself working in a similar way. He described how that happened to him:

> When you're first starting out, you just kind of latch on to somebody that you feel is more like you, and I connected with the nursery teacher because I felt that she had similar values to me and the things she did, I could see me being like that … It's about knowing how you are as a person, not necessarily with children. I think I went with the nursery teacher because she was more like me, not necessarily because of the way she taught children … We talked about the same things, not necessarily anything to do with education but, you know, we liked similar music, we watched similar things on TV, we read the same newspaper, those sorts of things and I thought, yes, I'd like to be like you.

It is interesting to see that, in this extract, Matthew mentions personal rather than professional values here and lists some of the social influences that he felt contributed to the ways in which he identified with his colleague. Another key mentor for Matthew was his first headteacher, and although he admits never to have seen her teach, he thought that 'her enthusiasm for teaching and learning was quite infectious' and felt that her enthusiasm 'rubbed off' on him.

> Even when she was bogged down in headteachery things, she always made the time to come into your room and say how wonderful something is, and she was always really, really positive about what you were doing and what the children were doing. She was quite inspirational, really.

Clearly, being valued in this way and by a headteacher reinforced his own views and affirmed his practice.

Although both had mentioned parents as a key influence, my question about what else might be feeding into their practice, nourishing and sustaining them, caused them both to be at first unsure. However, they both have young children and when invited to consider if parenting and their children might have an influence on classroom practice, Matthew was quick to see a connection between his young son learning to talk and ways in which children in his class were learning English as an additional language.

> I'm not really doing anything much to help him learn to speak and he seems to be doing quite a good job by himself really … There's not much greater thing in life, really, is there, apart from learning to how to talk, and I know that I am doing things to help him but he's doing amazingly to learn by himself … I'm thinking a lot at the moment about

the children I'm teaching who have no English, and I'm thinking about how I can best help them and mixing it up with how Joe's learning to talk.

Matthew's awe at his son's competence in learning to speak is mirrored later in the way that he generally speaks very respectfully of all children and their competence as learners. It's also interesting to note how he refers to helping children rather than teaching children. With his confidence in his role in his son's success in learning to speak, Matthew's confidence in his teaching approach is apparently justified.

Janette was concerned about 'how things make sense' for her youngest child, reflecting on how

> she tries to make sense of things and how muddled she sometimes is even though I thought we'd all understood it perfectly clearly … I thought she'd understood and she knew but then she'll say something and I'll think, no, you didn't get that, did you, and it makes me reflect often about the high expectation I have of the children at nursery whose linguistic skills on the whole are not as advanced as my daughter's and yet somehow when I speak to them, because I've got my teachery hat on, I expect it to be taken on board.

This level of reflection, listening to children and then thinking carefully about what it means, is also very typical of the ways in which Janette works to understand the children in her care in the nursery. Janette also wanted to return to Matthew's reflection on his son's ability to develop language 'by himself' and wondered 'if we have such a big influence as we think we have as a teacher'. She claimed that 'we're encouraged to assume that children learn because of us, but I don't think they do really … I think we're a great hindrance and annoyance in their development, in their learning, for a lot of the time.' Matthew felt that the idea that children could do things for themselves was a 'brave' position for teachers to take, 'if I just butt out for a bit and it's probably better for me butting out'. He also added that he trusted children, and that his levels of trust came from experience.

Both teachers said little about teaching or learning content, until particularly questioned about planning towards the end of the session. Even here the conversation reverted quickly back to principles of planning and practice. The conversation turned to how both teachers accounted for learning, that is how they planned and recorded learning. Both teachers use a range of strategies for recording what the children were doing and learning, for example, adults made notes of events; photographed children and play and physical outcomes; and talked with children about what they were doing and what they were learning. Janette led this part of the conversation:

> We still have a notional backdrop of six bite-sized chunks of the curriculum that are our backdrop for the term … we plan a daily sessional basis, the

record for inside and outside and the staff rota'd for outside plan and record the next sessions from the threads of what has happened; but alongside that, key worker plans are usually planned weekly and evaluated daily, so each key worker plans the key worker time which is adult-directed but comes from children's learning and interests in that group.

Although from observation evidence it is clear that in Janette's nursery adult-directed time is minimal, it is clearly very carefully managed. I followed up this section of information with a subsidiary question, asking what exactly in the nursery is likely to have been pre-planned. Janette stated:

Usually the threads for three or four significant activities like ... that a child may have started to play doctors, so the next day we may plan to have an adult around in that area and have a lot of the doctors' resources out and available that are not usually around in that area and make suggestions and see if that play will spark off, or a child may have found a drinking straw in the workshop and be blowing bubbles in the water tray, so the following session we may have made plans to put bubble painting out to see if that would be ... so, make plans based on observations of what seems to catch the children's interests, based on observations of what has been noticed.

It seemed to me to be evident that resources were very carefully planned too, and Janette added that where adults were based was also planned. I assumed that the activities themselves were not preordained and Janette added to this:

We would plan which children we would probably encourage and invite to come to that but we wouldn't say what we would do. What we might do is plan for that more fully to happen during an adult-directed group time. So, for example, we might decide not to put bubble painting out during the session because of XY and Z but ... Sarah's group that that child was in might do bubble blowing where another group might do something else. And if that was a roaring success, we might leave it out the next session.

Matthew's nursery was similarly very carefully planned. In the same way that Janette's planning depended on close observation and response to the children's interests, Matthew described how this approach was taken on in his nursery:

I quite carefully plan for my directed time ... the first thing we do is directed activity in groups or in the whole group, depending on what we were doing; and then we do what I would call adult-initiated things that we had set out around the place, based on what we had seen the children doing previously; and then we would encourage them to have a go at the activities that we'd set up for them. They wouldn't have to do the activities but we'd have children, like Janette says, that we'd noticed them doing X, so it may be it's good for them to do Y. We'd have it out for them to do the next day or if not the next day, the day after and encourage them to do that; and then we kind of reflect on that alltogether or in little groups and then form the planning train ... I would plan how the adults would be supporting the children during that time, they might be observing or they might be playing with the children or alongside the children.

I then suggested that both teachers gave children a choice, inviting or encouraging children rather than instructing, insisting, directing or coercing in any way. It seemed to be important to gather some information about this, to find out why. The following is a connected extract from the transcript:

J: Because it goes back to that underpinning principle that I subscribe to that children learn best when they're interested and focused, and for such very young children that's when they choose what they do themselves, and it's very hard but not impossible ... And actually the quality of learning is an awful lot better visibly – you can visibly see their involvement level and their concentration level and even the outputs are so much higher quality and detailed if you don't overdirect them. If you overdirect them, then they comply because you're bigger than them most of the time, but they're not actually learning very much or it isn't evident that they're learning very much.

M: I think you need lots to do because they're 26 very different children in your class who are not all going to possibly want to do the thing that you might want them to do; why should they want to do that ... ? And even sometimes when you think, you know, when Janette was saying, they're blowing bubbles, then that might have been, that's it, that's all they need to do with bubbles because you might think OK, they're playing with bubbles now, but tomorrow I'll get them to do, I'll get them to do x with bubbles, but that might be that moment's gone; I couldn't care less about bubbles now, I've found out all I wanted to find out about bubbles today and tomorrow I want to find out about bricks or I want to ... so sometimes you can plan and that's important, but it doesn't always ...

J: But usually with 26 children, if it doesn't come off for the one that you thought it might, then you catch somebody else ... You build up a large bank of things that children like to do.

This is a fascinating interchange. Here, between two teachers who both believe strongly in children's choice and independence, is a slight difference in approach which might signify simply a superficial difference in classroom management but may signal a more fundamental difference. Janette refers twice to her caution not to 'overdirect' children, indicating that, in spite of her insistence on children's choices, that she may at times direct them. What is notable here about Matthew's extract is that he seems perfectly content to follow children's interests. His repeated 'I'll get them to do … ', I believe occurred because Matthew was listening to his own voice creating that prescriptive phrase. Matthew's next comment mentions 'schemas' for the first time, and without schemas being specifically referenced in the conversation, but he has clearly interpreted Janette's approach to be connected with schema theory and has begun to deconstruct it, suggesting that it might constrain children and their choices. Janette, in her next exchange, in part defends the idea, suggesting that it could be 'one way of understanding how children develop' but also that it can be overused. Although the use of schemas or not in understanding practice is interesting, as it does not appear from observations, video or further conversations to reflect a substantial difference in the way that either teacher relates to children, it will not be followed up as a theme in itself. At this stage, neither teacher is expressing an extreme view.

Observing Janette: 2

The second observation occurred midway during a session. Janette was seated on the floor next to a large low-sided container which held a mixture of damp sand and wood chippings. There were three boys present, two were 3 years old and one was just 4. The children were playing with dinosaurs. Two children were actively manipulating the dinosaurs and one mainly observed, cooperating but not actively collaborating. In all, the play had been sustained for one and a half hours, with the children continuously engaged and reportedly anxious to continue. I was present for the final 25 minutes of the play. During that time, Janette's attention was totally focused upon this small group of children and, while she only occasionally physically manipulated the dinosaurs, she appeared to be very much part of the play group. Any actions taken followed the lead provided by the children and were not independent of the children's narrated play actions.

On this second observation, Janette's narration was considerably less than on the first occasion although still evident. It may have been that the boys were sufficiently assertive in their play, single-minded in their collaborations, not to need any attempt to cohere the play or the storying and so her intentions in narration and the overall purpose for her presence were considerably different. It may otherwise have been that Janette had been independently reconsidering her role in play, following earlier conversations.

In order to make sense of her interactions in this section I have attempted to create categories of teacher talk and have given examples of each in Table 6.1. The categories were developed from the transcribed data and while this may not be a definitive list, they suited the play example quoted here.

Table 6.1 Categories of teacher talk

Category	Comment
Questioning	Who could this be?
	Which way has he got to go?
Doing the voices	I want my mummy
Helping	Can I help cover him?
Punctuating	Hurray!
Explaining	His tail looks like a snake though
Interpreting	I think he meant...
(for other children)	
Narrating	Oh no, he's lost his mummy
Mirroring	Child: He's waiting
	J: He is waiting...
Repeating	I've missed you, mummy
Problem setting and solving	There's not a path to get there – what shall we do?
	Shall we clear a path? Hurray, now they can go across.
Agreeing	Child: I need to move this away
	J: Ah yes
Commenting	What a polite dinosaur

It is notable that instructional dialogue is not evident in this example, nor in these kinds of storying narratives. Instead, modelling a range of cognitive acts through the talk categories above seems generally to be the case in these interactions. This pedagogy is far from a transmission model and closer to a social constructivist approach on a continuum of practice (see Corden 2000). These talk patterns also suggest a 'preparedness to act contingently' (ibid.: 112) which categorises the kinds of interactions in which Janette seems to most frequently engage and is particularly evident in her storying play. Further, Carter claims that 'Creativity is a matter of dialogue with others and the social and cultural contexts for creative language use need to be more fully emphasised' (2004: 11). The emphasis in Carter's recent research is on creativity in everyday language interactions and his charge here is particularly relevant in the nursery contexts being studied and accounts for the 'contingent' choices Janette makes in her interactions: 'Appreciation of literary and broader cultural variation can also be stimulated by reference to what learners already understand and can do in everyday interaction rather than by more deficit-related pedagogic paradigms' (ibid.: 213).

Janette appears to be alert to the possibility of what can be created or generated from play, only rarely initiating, intervening or leading, although I have observed her offering broader interpretations or helping to weave in other children's versions.

At one point in the play, when all dinosaurs had been effectively buried in the sand/chippings, Janette 'wondered' if they had slept for long enough. The child she addressed, however, was undaunted by the question and covered them over even more, insisting that they slept on. The children in Janette's nursery are encouraged towards being independent decision-makers, autonomous in their play, and more evidence of this was demonstrated as the dinosaur play began to extend beyond the boundaried container. Wooden blocks were introduced by one child and a housing complex began to be constructed for the dinosaurs next to the container and pathways and bridges built for them to reach the houses. As a child built the houses, he sang the 'Bob the Builder' theme tune; his singing was incidental – a backcloth to his building. Another child, while playing was talking through his play:

Child: ... hiding crocodiles, all asleep under sand.
J: I can see his tail.
Child: maybe he's got to go *through* it.
            [reference to 'I'm going on a Bear Hunt' story]

Both are examples of casual intertextuality, which itself denotes an interesting developmental element of literacy learning. However, there was no evidence that this was seen as especially significant on this occasion and this fact was woven into later conversation.

Janette warned the children that the session was coming to an end and two children began to tidy away, with others who had come to help. The play session ended and an adult-directed section of the morning was about to begin. The third dinosaur playing child, child 3, had in the meantime casually sat at a nearby table and had drawn a map of the dinosaur complex that had been created. I had assumed that Janette had not seen this as she had begun to read a story to another child. However, as a colleague in the nursery collected a small group of children to take them on a planned walk along adjoining streets, Janette asked her to include child 3 in the walk and to include conversation relating to direction and map making. Janette's attention to the children and constant awareness of their actions, behaviour, intentions and conversation are always evident in her behaviour in the nursery. This example of continuous formative assessment illustrates Janette's attention to and understanding of what she describes as 'the learner's point of need'. I believe this to be an intuitive act, representative of intuitive practice, informed by knowledge of the child, children in general, child development and, importantly, in tune with the child's intentions and interests.

Interviewing Janette: 2

Immediately following the observation, Janette and I discussed her role, what she believed she was doing with the children during this storying play event. We began by talking about the adult's role in play and Janette felt that her role was to be 'one step ahead ... feeding in other ideas that they might use later.' Although it was also true that she sometimes stood back to observe, Janette said emphatically, 'If they've got you there playing with them, then you're there playing and you need to play.' The level of commitment to the status of play and the significance of the teacher as player to children is evident in the emphatic nature of this response. This idea of the adults being simply of use to children is repeated often in conversations with both Janette and Matthew. Janette tried to articulate what difference she felt an adult's presence made to the play and what her purposes were. While she clearly acknowledged that often there were many times when there are not 'enough adults to go round and they haven't got anyone with them', the importance of there being such adult-free times is also stressed when Janette agrees that an adult's role is frequently governed by an agenda. She accounts for that:

> I suppose my agenda is that you're trying to get the play to be more sustained, more complex, aren't you, in those broad terms ... but not in terms of maths, language, attaching it to anything, not in a way that overtakes what they're interested in, because some of the things I said nobody reacted to, so, you think, keep quiet for a minute, and I suppose that's why I mirror and repeat because you're trying to give weight to what they're saying, that you've heard it and it's important in this game and you're giving the message – I'm listening, 'Oh, so he's underneath', so you're hearing that, but you also add a bit on or inflect your voice a bit differently, don't you, so you'll go, 'Is he asleep? He's been asleep a long while', so hopefully it'll push them on a bit more. I think that's what you do, isn't it?

There is an immense subtlety in this kind of teacher–child interaction, as well as deeply held knowledge and understanding. For example, in order not to 'overtake' what the children are interested in, a teacher would need to listen to, attend to and acknowledge that child's subject of interest. They would also need to understand when and how to encourage 'sustained and more complex' play and be very sensitive to the flow of the play and their own role in it. For example, Janette continued to talk about how one of the children was instructing her in the play and how she was prepared to be led by him:

> Child 1 this morning – you need these and you need to put them there – and you do it, don't you really ... I was interested in what he needed me for but he didn't follow it up, I obviously didn't respond in the right way to him because it didn't continue. I took the hippos and I was waiting for him to tell me what they were to do, because I was aware that I had been doing a lot of, you know, 'Ooh, I wonder If I can ... ' I hope I wasn't taking the lead, I hope we were leading together. He didn't tell me, maybe he was wanting more of a story

input but I was holding back ... It's so difficult to think about because afterwards you're trying to put a reason on why you behaved in a particular way.

One of the important comments to consider here is Janette's idea that the child may have wanted more of a story input. Clearly there is an ongoing tension for her between the idea of waiting and following children in their storymaking and introducing and suggesting. Janette acknowledges the intuitive manner in which she performs and the difficulty of taking a retrospective view. But it is interesting to also note in this extract that Janette is, even amidst the storymaking activity itself, acknowledging the complexities in her role. Janette pursued the idea of accountability as another part of her role at this stage in the conversation and attended in this way to an unspoken concern from the observation about the significance or not of a literacy development (the intertextuality mentioned earlier):

> Just before you came, Lynn zipped round with a camera, just as an aide-mémoire really. And if I write up some of their learning stories ... then I will be able to, if I choose to, map against literacy – that was comparative literacy – I feel I have got that broad agenda to translate into Early Years Foundation-speak, that's my agenda, not theirs, isn't it?

Her questions are, of course, rhetorical. I asked then if the children were unaware of this, that is Janette's agenda, during play and this caused a little apparent discomfort:

> Well, they might be, and they probably are – that sounds as if you're tricking them but it's not like that – they might be aware because I might say something like 'Oh, that was really good counting, you've counted all those numbers up to 10', had they done that – there you're reinforcing. If they've all been hiding and you've lost some, then you might say ... but only if that would be appropriate for their play. So if they've lost them all and they need to count them, I might suggest they count them. I'm told what to do a lot by the children.

The whole idea of influencing children, of it somehow feeling slightly dishonest or manipulative, was worrying for Janette. As the reflective practitioner that she clearly is, Janette had been churning over one of our previous discussions about why teachers do the things they do, and she made a connection at this point in the conversation. Her response is typically forthright and committed:

> After you said last time about my agenda I was a bit narked. I thought, oh damn. I didn't like the idea of me having an agenda and my values

and what have you – and you're right, I flipping well have! And I kind of didn't want to have one, if you know what I mean. I was blithely pretending I'm neutral and I'm not at all, but nobody is … it's shaped by your knowledge base and your beliefs and all those things.

The influences of this kind of research project are clear in this short extract and it is fascinating to hear from Janette how she had been churning over ideas that had been raised. Because both teachers are being asked to uncover their professional intentions and influences and articulate their beliefs in relation to their practice, inevitably values are laid bare and the resulting tension is evident in Janette's responses.

I think we were talking about whose values and whose stuff was I, the practitioner, transmitting onto the children … and I just am shocked to realise that it's mine – mine within a mixture of society's and the different personalities here, because it's tempered by everybody here; and at the end of the day it's mine, and that led me to think, well, 'How dare I do such a thing, who am I to say that those children should have my values?' and that just worried me a bit and that's scary because I might believe that my values are true and just and right but actually someone might with the opposite values believe that theirs are true and right and just.

Janette agonises briefly here at the stark realisation that not only is she not neutral but that no-one else is either, 'because there's all sorts of crazy folk'. However, her professional self quickly takes hold as she rationalises what she considers to be a distinction:

I can't change the Janette-ness of Janette but I can be aware of it, you know, and you can have that metalanguage to take it out and think about it, can't you, so that you are aware that perhaps some of the ways that a child responds, because if Linda had been there, when Linda was there, the children she was interacting with were interacting with her differently because she is Linda; so you have to be aware of the influence you have or the impact you have. I don't think you can do much about it other than give it its proper … acknowledge it and give it its weight.

Janette has apparently resolved the issue for herself in her acknowledgement of the influence and impact that she may have and her ability to gather a perspective on this by adopting a critically reflexive stance. At this point I moved towards an element of the previous conversation with Matthew that I wanted to check back with her. This was the difference between her role in the nursery and her parental role at home, during play:

Yes, I think it's the same. I always try to play as well. You know how, sometimes, when you play with children, and it is appropriate sometimes, you are just the presence and the sounding board, aren't you? And I'm not saying that's never appropriate, sometimes that is appropriate, but some people don't get past that.

Her response that it is the same is interesting, but I believe that Janette is referring not to the relationship in the role but to her role as player and so the next sentence is the qualification, 'I always try to play as well'. The other very relevant part of the extract here to look at is Janette's description, that some people are merely 'a presence and the sounding board'. This is an accurate description of the very limited role that it is possible for an adult to take in a child's play, without becoming completely immersed. While she is not totally dismissive of this, the similarity between her own roles at home and at school lies precisely there: Janette plays, she is a player.

It seemed appropriate to extend the topic here towards one of the continuous threads in all conversations: the importance of relationships and any potential connection between parent–child relationships and teacher–child relationships. In order to better explain her position, Janette offered a brief, recent example:

There's a child here in the afternoon who is relatively new ... you'd love her, a real strong character, and the other day I was at the computer with another child and she wanted my attention, so she actually climbed over my arm and she squidgilled down onto my lap in just the way [her own daughter] would have done and I thought to myself, now that's a good relationship because you are comfortable and confident to actually behave like you would to a parent ... she climbed over and that was enough, that was all she wanted and she sat there for quite a while, and I suppose in that kind of way I suppose you feel, ah yes, this is good stuff.

Janette's coined term here 'squidgilled' illustrates perfectly the kind of movement a small child might make to ease themselves into an adult's presence. It is also a kind of familial expression, more readily associated with an emotionally based relationship, which is exactly what Janette is honouring. This is an important extract as it reflects the nature of Janette's connection with the children in her care, that she is sufficiently sensitive to appreciate the physical and emotional needs of individual children and content to acknowledge and accept the physical relationship that at times appears to be necessary for young children. Janette does not appear to be self-conscious in her attitude here towards physical and emotional contact, despite common concern and many public debates that this may not be an appropriate aspect of a professional role with children. Janette's ability to tune into individual children's needs and development is further evidenced when she reflects on whether or not they have been helped by whatever development or learning activity that has been undertaken. She says, rather enthusiastically:

> You can see it in his eyes, that this is what he needs and what he wants, can't you, you can see by the look on his face, whereas for other children it wasn't what they needed at that time, so they've chosen something else, but you can tell I'm getting it right just for this minute.

I asked what to 'see it in his eyes' actually meant and Janette described it as 'a connection' and a 'ha ha moment', 'that kind of I know what you mean, you know what I mean look' and an 'I like this, I want to play more look', or an 'I know that you know that you know that I know' look. As she defines these terms in her own way, it is clear that Janette is drawing on countless experiences with young children in order to shape her descriptive responses. Here again, Janette really begins to search for meaning and for the connection between parent and teacher of young children. With her own children, Janette said 'you know what makes them tick'. She goes on to rhetorically ask, reflecting herself without prompts:

> But what's that about? It's about being someone very important, being close to and all those sorts of things which is the same as what you're trying to recreate really. Somebody said, didn't they, that you're just trying to be like a good parent really, which is a bit dismissive, but if you actually unpick what being a parent means, it's similar behaviour, isn't it, and it's about that relationship and knowing that person as an individual. And it's about knowing them, knowing them.

Although the recent work of Katz (2007) seeks to identify the distinction between mothering and teaching, Janette is identifying two intentional aspects of teaching children, and young children in particular, that are similar; that is the need to fill an important space in children's everyday lives, 'being someone very important' and the need to know the child, a point on which she lays particular emphasis in this extract. Of course, as Katz also claims, the differences exist between a parent who behaves often spontaneously, sometimes irrationally and always affectively and a teacher who is intentional in her work with children; electing to become important in children's lives and choosing to know children well. My study is focusing on two teachers who have specified these aspects of their role, although many other teachers, policy-makers and politicians do not.

Janette ends this session by attempting to draw together threads of the conversation and offering a concluding statement:

> When you're meeting the child's needs, you're meeting your own need to have the child's needs met, that's your need as a teacher, isn't it, your

professional need ... from that comes that reciprocal relationship perhaps, that's rewarding in itself, isn't it?

Throughout, Janette has couched some of her statements as questions although they are invariably rhetorical and not a way of seeking approval or reassurance. Janette prefaced each session with a version of 'I know you're going to ask me hard questions', although smiling as if relishing the opportunity, and perhaps this is worth considering later when discussing implications from this study. Her responses are evidence of how earnestly she has attempted to respond to the challenge offered to define her role, her work, her relationships and her self.

Observing Matthew: 2

The observation was midway during an afternoon session. Most of the children were outside as it was a bright winter day. While the nursery is not well equipped or resourced, the outdoor space is large and includes a paved, covered area as well as a large fenced grass space. There are trees and large fixed climbing apparatus as well as play houses. The children also had a table for small world, wheeled toys and a sand tray. When I arrived, Matthew was holding a shovel while children swept leaves and wheelbarrowed them onto the grass and under a tree. Matthew was helping them to decide the best place to pile the leaves. He then moved to the sand tray and played quietly with a group of children there. At the appropriate time, Matthew warned the children that the session was soon to end and helped to tidy up resources with the children. In the final section of the session, the children were in two groups, half with the teaching assistant and half with Matthew. They had a review of their independent play session.

   On this occasion it was difficult to take notes during the session. While they were outside, I was co-opted by the children to help sweep the leaves, and during the review session, I found it very difficult to understand them, in part because of the children's language delay and in part as some had very little active English. It may have been that, as an outsider, I was not quickly able to tune into the children's versions of spoken English, in much the same way that adults other than parents do not often clearly understand babies and young children in everyday home contexts. Matthew's own review of the session, however, is very detailed and confirms my general overview.

Interviewing Matthew 2

In order to prompt this conversation, Matthew was asked whether he had an agenda when he played with children, for example, when he played in the sand, and how he saw his role within play contexts:

> I think it's important not to have an agenda sometimes, when I go to play with children, because otherwise I think I start doing and saying things that I want, that's not necessarily what they want or where they're going or what they've even thought about. Sometimes I just go, and this afternoon I just went and started playing alongside them ... I just started playing and waiting for K to engage with me and sometimes I'll engage straight away but this afternoon I was waiting to see, to give them time to use me if they wanted to or ignore me if they wanted to – use me to bounce ideas off, tell me something, help them, explain something, be there as another body.

There is a very close similarity here to Janette's view of her role in the dinosaur play, that it is appropriate sometimes to wait for the children to lead them, the teachers, into the play action. Matthew, like Janette earlier, is making a very significant and unusual comment here; he suggests that a teacher can be used by children for a variety of reasons, rather than the teacher using children for, for example, performative reasons. This aspect of their work clearly distinguishes these two teachers from others in the profession and is of paramount importance. He also suggests that his role grows out of his engagement rather than the nature of the engagement growing out of his role. This topsy-turvy approach is typical of Matthew's approach to teaching and his insistence that his knowledge of what to do during play is found within the play and during the play.

> Sometimes I'll think something's there, the moment's there, that we can maybe move something on or a little bit of something that we can achieve there ... but other times it will just be a case of whatever happens will happen and the children will take it where they'll take it.

On the surface, this may seem to be a very relaxed notion of teaching. However, it becomes evident through the conversation that there are very subtle layers – of planning, of observation, of intervention. In relation to resources, Matthew claims that 'We've got things set up for the children to engage with, that's providing them with the structure, the bit of structure, that they might need.' As an observer, it is difficult to see and analyse where his interventions are occurring. However, Matthew talked through his play session and it was possible to extract very significant points of intervention.

> K initially was trying to fill a pot but the pot was broken ... and she tried to make a sandcastle with it and the pots were there if they wanted to but it wasn't really happening and she wasn't really getting frustrated but she tried it a couple of times and so at that stage, I did give her another pot, or just put it near, I didn't pass it to her, I just put it closer

to her and she swapped pots and tried to make one with a pot that wasn't broken and had more success.

What it is interesting to look at here is Matthew's ability again to wait, to observe, before his intervention, and this of course rested upon his security in his own knowledge of the individual child and her levels of frustration. It seemed very important for Matthew to make clear that he neither instructed nor directed K but instead made a resource available to K to enable a successful outcome. His tentative role, in my view, is unusual and deliberate and dependent on the pace that Matthew applies to his work, neither rushed nor intrusive. In the second example, Matthew described what he called 'social guidance' during the sand play:

> One of the children took a scoop from one of the other children and she was right in the middle of using it. M was a bit upset; she wouldn't necessarily do anything about it, she would accept that. So my role there was to give her the idea that you don't have to accept that, it's not acceptable and it's not something you have to put up with in school. And so I provided her with somebody to help her out of that situation ... I said to R, M was using that, do you think that was fair? Actually R didn't in the end, he gave it back but then he was thinking, well, I haven't got a scoop, what am I supposed to do here?, and so I was able to say, well, this isn't a scoop, but you can use it like one, and he was quite happy with that. So, if I hadn't been there, M would have carried on regardless, R would have been quite happy because he'd got what he wanted, M wouldn't have been but I wouldn't have helped M to begin to stand up a bit for herself or helped R to think, that's not on, not a good way to carry out social relationships.

It is important to remember that our conversation was occurring immediately following the session and that Matthew is drawing on the previous activities with the children to demonstrate his roles in play. He has not had time to prepare or to even know what was to be discussed. In view of this, his ability to draw out of particular scenarios a relevant aspect and analyse it is quite remarkable. The point to note in this extract is that this is a significantly more pro-active role than Matthew's earlier description of himself as being 'used' by the children. Nevertheless, he is still sustaining a relatively low profile adult role, asking – 'do you think that was fair?', suggesting – 'you can use it like one', supporting – 'helped M to begin to stand up a bit for herself', 'that's not on'. There is a subtlety to this kind of interaction and it illustrates well Matthew's commitment to the development of relationships, teacher and child, child and child, in his nursery. Also, each child and each event appear to potentially demand a different response: 'G did start throwing the sand up, so at that point I said, giving it a bit of a moment to see if it ended naturally, no, so then I said, oh, is that nice?, no, so then it should stop.' Matthew is very clear that roles interchange, 'then I go into that role' but his emphasis on 'good, decent relationships' is unwavering.

> I don't quite know how to say it but something about the social aspect of it that ... if I hadn't been there, there wouldn't have been quite as much interaction between the children, if they weren't going necessarily to talk to each other. They were coming through me and then they did start together but they'd been through me first. I don't think that would necessarily have happened without me there, but it did happen because I was there.

So, as well as being 'another child almost', 'standing next to them, sitting next to them' and being 'a partner in their play', Matthew is also claiming a role as a talk mediator and a social guide. He illustrated how he was able to correct behaviour, support a change in behaviour and develop talk. Matthew provided an example of further variants on his teaching role, a model at play, demonstrating rather than leading in the following example:

> One of the children was having difficulty trying to get the sand out of the yoghurt pot but it wasn't coming ... she picked it up, it was still in there, so she put it back down again, so I did mine and gave it a tap, so we talked a bit about just give it a tap. And so she gave it a great big wallop, quite a huge wallop, and took it off and it just went phew ... the sand went and so I showed my tap, tap one and she filled it up again and so I just said, 'Why don't you just try and give it a tap, be a bit more gentle with it – if you want it to be a sandcastle, be a bit gentle.' She didn't particularly want it to be a castle and just gave it another whack but the time after that, after she'd thought about it, she filled it up with sand again put it down gently, gave it a tap and it did come out with a reasonable sandcastle, then she repeated it.

Again, the pace of response that Matthew describes is a feature of his work with children. He speaks slowly although his speech is not slow, responds in a measured and very deliberate way and there is no sense of haste in his interactions with children. When they speak, he listens with attention and is very aware of the relationships he is building with the children:

> I'm engaging in, or trying to engage in, a proper relationship ... so that we were actually enjoying the play together. So it wasn't me the teacher, K child – we were playing together so we were talking ... We made a hand print and we enjoyed it together. Not, you know, we made a print because the sand is wet, if you tried that with dry sand ... then, if you're not careful, then the magic stops. K's enjoying the moment with the

wet sand, she doesn't particularly want, I didn't think she wanted to know then that there's dry sand there, and it wouldn't have worked.

Matthew's idea of 'enjoying the moment' with children is unusual for a teaching professional. He is not considering progress or next steps or learning needs, but simply servicing the moment. He says that 'the greatest thing that I do now is just being another person there, but a grown-up person'. It is important to note here that the position that Matthew is taking is both thoughtful and deliberate, assigning himself a role to take, in play.

The conversation included a discussion about teacher talk and Matthew was concerned about overuse of questioning: 'Really I've been on so many things, I've thought so much about questioning recently and now I'm very careful about how I do it and I try not to do it all the time.' These comments serve to demonstrate the level of reflective awareness in his own contributions. Matthew was also concerned not to be too suggestive during play: 'If I started questioning and suggesting, then it might have gone in a wonderful direction but it was going in a perfectly wonderful direction as it was'. Again, this shift of the balance of power from the teacher to the children is unusual. Particularly significant and unusual too is his acknowledgement of the worth of children's chosen routes or directions, whereas teacher's choices are usually given precedence. Matthew had begun to temper this way of working with a new approach, in his view. In this extract he is describing his talk when he started playing with the sand:

> I talked about what I was doing when I first arrived – giving a bit of a commentary about what I was doing, and commenting on the things that the children were doing. Since talking with Janette and you, I have started doing that a bit more, I've started narrating things a bit more ... there are lots of children here who need a lot more encouragement to talk, to talk about what they're doing. I don't know if they have that skill, that language, and so like Janette did, it's almost giving them language so I'm trying to do that at the moment.

Matthew is very open here about the influence of our conversations on his practice and his reflective approach is illustrated as he considers the benefits to be gained from trying a new way of working. He is so evidently very aware of the needs of the children and has found this kind of storying to be a vehicle to support children with a limited active vocabulary in English, for various reasons.

Matthew's final comments, when asked to describe himself as a teacher, underline the threads that have been woven through every conversation:

> I just think it's about relationships ... I think I'm a teacher who is very worried about the relationship he has with the children, not worried but very high priority. I think about it a lot and spend a lot of time making

sure we have proper relationships, almost equal relationships, so that I can go and play with them and its all very natural; not 'Oh, I've got to perform because Matthew's here or I've got to behave because Matthew's here. I just want, oh, he's turned up, we'll just carry on' ... That all sounds a bit trendy and lefty, doesn't it, but then anybody can come in here and see these children, they're behaving, they're interested and engaged; even when they're not engaged they're browsing or thinking about what they're having for tea; but then they're being reasonable, social, sociable children who are being kind and sharing and have good decent social relationships with the adults and the children and that's because of the ethos we've created here ... and at the moment they don't feel the need to do things that people might see as misbehaving, there are too many other things to do you know, why would I ... so I am doing my teacher thing as well but that's because of what we've created and the time we've invested talking about those sorts of things and creating the right sort of environment. And a lot of that's down to my personality and the way I like to do it as well and the way I like it to be ... it's about having high expectations of them and wanting them to achieve as much as they possibly can and more than that.

The picture that Matthew paints of himself is of a very committed professional who has invested a great deal into his practice and who feels that the essence of his work with children is forged on the strength of relationships that have been built and sustained in an environment of trust and support. Layered upon this non-negotiable bedrock of strong relationships, there is clear evidence of a questioning, reflective and adaptable practice, responsive to the needs of children and servicing the intentions of children at play. Matthew is not unaware of his responsibilities as a teacher. It is worth noting in the extract above that he lists his investments, importantly in relationships, but also in the environment, the ethos, in conversations with colleagues, in raising expectations of both behaviour and achievement. When asked to list the key roles and functions he employs during play, Matthew includes: player, model, commentator, partner, questioner, language support, listener, watcher, note taker, pivotal support/integrator, practical guide, social guide, challenger and suggestion maker, and claims that there may be more.

Finally, in answer to an enquiry about how 'systematic' his work might be, a term often used by politicians, Matthew replies:

I think it is systematic because I do monitor very, very carefully by observing and talking to the children about where they are ... [with] the rest of the nursery team, we talk about next steps but it all gets, you know, 'Is it the next step and how do you know it's the next step?', and would that really be the next thing and perhaps they need to spend the next two weeks doing exactly the same thing. But can you write that on a next step, that they need to do the same thing for the next two weeks ... they've only just started doing that and they're alright but they do need, they can do the next thing but where is the next thing?

While superficially this may appear to be a very loose response, Matthew's puzzlement about current policy about ensuring progress, his self-reflection, his critical stance and his complete commitment – 'someone who thinks almost 24/7 about my practice' – are all evidenced in this extract as he struggles to make sense of what Janette has described earlier as 'next steps malarkey'! However, what is demonstrated is that he is very clear about the fact that he observes and monitors children in his nursery and engages in conversations with colleagues about the children and their achievements.

Categories of data

Following the second research conversations, a system of open coding was applied to the transcripts. These categories were chosen from attempts to group or characterise responses from a reading of the transcripts. In this kind of flexible design study, where organic research structures were being used, it became necessary to allow themes to emerge rather than presuppose where the focus might be. In this case, the four categories below developed out of the conversations, appeared frequently and could therefore be assumed to be of significance to the two teachers. The texts were then trawled to discover where examples could be found of them. The four categories are:

1 Content responses (e.g. the children choose to ...).
2 Emotive language (e.g. it feels right, I learned that it matters what you do).
3 Reference to self, selfhood, self-making (e.g. I'm the teacher I am because of who I am).
4 Reference to mentors or communities of practice (e.g. I think it was just being amongst people who talked about children all the time ...).

The examples given in Table 6.2 represent the categories of responses. The first category, content responses, was among the hardest to clearly identify as the only time that content was mentioned it grew into a principled response relating rather more to some of the other categories, as will be evident below.

The least significant responses for the purposes of this study relate to organisation of content and preparation of materials. The rest of the examples listed become highly significant to the analyses in this study as they relate to personal values, personal constructs and mentors and influential people who have been important at some point in their lives. The content responses relating to the bubble activity, discussed in more detail elsewhere in the study, are, however, significant in their relationship to the ways that children's development is being understood and the impact that has on planning in both settings.

Table 6.2 Categories and examples

Category	Example	Why important
1 Content response	• A lot of it was cutting up pieces of paper and stuff that we wouldn't perhaps do now	Describing community activities at early career stage
	• It was about preparing and thinking through and being organised	
	• A child may have found a drinking straw in the workshop and be blowing bubbles ... so the following session we may have made plans to put bubble painting out to see	Describing planning content and adult interpretation of children's intentions
	• You know, when Janette was saying they're blowing bubbles, then that might have been that's it, that's all they need to do with bubbles because you might think, OK, they're playing with bubbles now but tomorrow I'll get them to do, *I'll get them to do* X with bubbles but that might be that moment's gone. I couldn't care less about bubbles now, I've found out all I wanted to find out about bubbles today and tomorrow I want to find out about bricks or I want to ...	Challenging popular view of plans and defending child's intentionality
	• I think you need lots to do because they're 26 very different children in your class who are not all going to possibly want to do the thing that you might want them to do, why should they?	Defending resourcing as planning and child's right to choose
	• She says she can remember my face lighting up, and we instantly knew, ha ha, this is the place for me	Intuitive connections with colleagues
2 Emotive language relating to how it feels	• I've come across things and I've thought, Oh blimey, yeah, oh right, oh flipping heck, and they make a change in you, you read something or you meet somebody or you talk to somebody, and you think hurrah I'm not an idiot at all, I am on the right path	Intuitive connections with ideas and connections with others
	• It's a bit vague, isn't it, they either sit right or they don't	Intuitive connections

Table continued on next page.

Table 6.2 (continued)

Category	Example	Why important
	• You just get a feeling, yes, that's OK, that's the right thing to be doing right now	Intuitive connections
3 Reference to self, selfhood, self-making, etc.	• I think it goes back to my values and beliefs then	Influences and trust in core values
	• Where they come from don't ask me	Trust in self
	• Ultimately, to some extent it's always yourself	Between self and professional self
	• You believe it, you believe it and you're not easily dissuaded from it	Own resources
	• It's about knowing how you are as a person, not necessarily with children	Professional identity
	• I feel like I'm nourishing myself at the moment	Knowledge of self and bigger picture of schooling
	• I think that's quite brave though, you have to be quite brave as a teacher to think that they can, they will do things for themselves, if I just butt out for a bit and it's probably better for me butting out	Trust in children
4 Reference to mentors and communities of practice	• It's come from a big run of very positive very committed interactions with people	People matter – early influences in connection with personal interactions
	• It was just being amongst people who talked about children all the time and who spent time and effort	Shared interest – professional
	• That's the way my dad talks to my children now, the way I talk to children, I suppose	Family mentor
	• Everybody's included, we do things for everybody, and I suppose that's the way I was brought up	Family mentor
	• There was the first person in the nursery ... and everything I did in Reception or tried to do was based around what I saw her doing	Early career professional mentor
	• I got quite a lot of how I didn't want to do things and then lots of things I did want to, you know, I thought, I'll take that or not take that, but that's what you do, isn't it?	Intuitive choices

Table continued on next page.

Table 6.2 (continued)

Category	Example	*Why important*
	• When you're first starting out, you just kind of latch on to somebody that you feel is more like you and I connected with the nursery teacher because I felt she had similar values to me, and the things that she did. I could see me being like that	Early career personal/ professional connections and shared values
	• I never saw her teach, I just heard her talk about teaching and just her enthusiasm for teaching and learning was quite infectious ... she was always so enthusiastic about everything and that rubbed off on me	Inspirational managers
	• She was quite inspirational really	
	• It's got to be your parents and how you grew up, and your friends and family and your family relationships	Family mentors

Summary

The teachers have identified clearly the importance of early career mentors and their families on the ways that they interact and behave with children in their care. They have both interrogated their own practice thoroughly to determine what they are doing, how they are doing it and for what purposes. They have also scrutinised their own intentions and values to search for influences and significant elements impacting on their professional lives. Their responses have been categorised into some key themes – content responses, emotive language use, reference to selfhood, self-making, and reference to mentors and inspiration. Of these four, content responses are the rarest, often thinner, creating less dynamic response between the two teachers.

In the current policy context described in early chapters, where teaching is often said to be more technical in nature, it seems that these two teachers are contradicting this pattern. From observations, video evidence and discussion, both teachers appear to operate on 'the plane of the personal' (Peters 1966) and are occupied with who they are, who the children are and the points of contact and conversation rather than with elements of progression in subject areas. They exhibit, in practice and in reflection, the ability 'to assert their own voices, while still being able to encourage [children] to affirm, tell, and retell their personal narratives by exercising their own voices' (Giroux 1987: 23). In Meek's discussion of Paolo Freire's inspirational texts, she identifies some educational practices as 'basic' or 'functional' and describes these brilliantly as the 'thinner gruel of educational nourishments'. With this in mind, the work of the teachers in this study, described above, clearly offers a rich diet to the children in their care.

Key elements in this chapter are:

1 Both appeared to be engaging in this kind of reflexive act for the first time.
2 The ability of both teachers to clearly interrogate their own practice, values and beliefs and to articulate significant areas, questions and dilemmas.
3 They seemed to be committed, to both their professional experiences and their responses and demonstrated the 'commitment to engage in such discourse in relation to one's own knowledge and one's values that ... constitutes the heart of true professionalism' (Furlong 2000: 27).
4 Their responses were categorised as containing: content information, emotive language, reference to selfhood and the inspiration of mentors.
5 Both teachers appeared to operate in 'the plane of the personal'.
6 Neither teacher fitted the 'technicist' model often quoted.

The next chapter analyses the conversations, the data, in more detail and begins to exemplify some key attributes demonstrated by the teachers.

Chapter 7

Who are these teachers and what are they doing?

'I'm the teacher I am because I'm the person I am'

The kind of pedagogy demonstrated in the classrooms of the two teachers is based upon a combination of thoughtful and thorough resourcing with demonstrable respect for children's intentions, interests and motivations. It includes close consideration of their physical, social and emotional needs. Into this mix, the teachers deliberately insert high levels of adult interaction. The interactions take on a range of forms, are frequently determined moment-by-moment according to context and the children involved, and are often intuitively based and may be spontaneously constructed. The range of interactions include mediating, instructing, narrating, participating, conversing, talking (in all its forms), problem-solving, listening, voicing and co-creating. While this does not pretend to be a fully inclusive list, it forms categories within which other types of interaction may be contained. For example, 'participating' may be evidenced as play, cooperative endeavours, resourcing, receiving, physical presence or addressivity.

This kind of pedagogy demands depth of knowledge and high levels of skills from those involved, along with physical and emotional stamina, tolerance, maturity and professionalism. All of these attributes are evidenced in both teachers' selves, demonstrated in their responses, and in their practice. They both present a quietly determined, self-confident approach and an ability to stretch towards both inner and outer motivations to search for the causes of, and the nourishment for, the high levels of personal investment evident in their work with children in their care. The nature of this reflexive practice will be further considered later in this section.

Their knowledge

In their conversations, the teachers displayed extensive knowledge, covering a range of fundamental elements relating to their practice. The nature of this 'knowledge' (which could be described as subject knowledge if the subject is early years education) can be deconstructed to include knowledge of the following broad areas, which will be separately considered:

- play as a site for learning;
- children and childhood;
- the children in their care;
- families and communities;
- government priorities, statutory requirements and the specified curriculum.

Play as a site for learning

In both the classrooms the *idea* of play is completely accepted as the context where children will learn. The maximum amount of time possible is given to children for them to play. The nursery classrooms entirely consist of play resources, play areas and ranges of possibilities for the children to play. There are consistent, fixed areas and flexible spaces as well as opportunities for change, resources to be added, moved, transported by the children and adapted. There are routines, but these are also flexible.

In both nurseries, everything – space, resources, routines, time, adults and interactions – are all arranged to best fit the perceived day-to-day needs of the children; their physical, social, emotional and cognitive needs. The adults mostly follow the children's lead, their interests and their intentions while at play. Janette's comment here is significant in understanding her place in children's world of play, 'the more our interactions fit in with the child, the more likely that they will be of use to the child in developing and extending, understanding whatever it is they are exploring'. It is this idea that adults need to be present in order to be *of use to children at play* that is of importance and it is also evident in Matthew's responses, 'I was waiting to see, to give them time *to use me* if they wanted to or ignore me if they wanted to – *use me* to bounce ideas off, tell me something, help them, explain something, be there as another body.' In these practices, the teachers are of use to children in their conceptual development as well as physically. They both, at different times, emphasise that they *help* children. This may sound simplistic and basic but it is in fact a very significant idea and it appears to form the bedrock of their practice; they are both clear that they are there to service children's play. This is not an idle or a passive role, however, although significantly different from the instructive, management role that many teachers of young children adopt. The evidence of the teachers' own words indicate that it is an informed choice, based on experience, information from a range of sources and their deeply reflexive approach to all aspects of their work.

Children and childhood

Both Janette and Matthew have clearly constructed views about children and childhood. These constructions include a deep level of respect for children as individuals who are operating within an inclusive learning community at the pace which their teachers believe to be appropriate. Janette valued lessons learned from her father about how to treat children, 'something about belonging and being part ... and treating children as worthy'. Both learned lessons about learning from observing their own children.

They are clear that children are themselves able to learn and to use a meta-language to take part in conversations relating to constructed understandings through play. Their responses to the question 'What do you think early education is for?' emphasise their understanding that early childhood is a stage for children to enjoy, rather than a stepping stone to the next key stage in children's development:

> Helping them to enjoy now, not preparing them; helping them find things they might like to explore, didn't explore as confidently as they might; take more risks. Creating a place where they can develop decent human relationships.
>
> (Matthew)

> It's about helping children be who they are, explore their strengths; being with them to make sense, discovering what's going on; being comfortable with who they are; helping children to have more control over their own lives; more ability to be more powerful.
>
> (Janette)

In these constructions, Janette and Matthew identify their roles as helping, resourcing and accompanying children on their educational journeys. Evident in their responses too is the notion that children are equipped to learn when provided with opportunities, space, time and support, but essentially it is the children themselves who are doing the learning, making their own sense, creating their own identities and taking control of their lives and their learning. Janette's conviction, expressed here, summarises this idea: 'It's about seeing it as their learning, it belongs to them, and I have a role in helping to build learning and development, but it isn't mine to build, it's theirs.' This conception of the autonomy of young learners and the volitional nature of learning is very unusual. Teachers appear to have become accustomed, through submission to government pressures, SATs and Ofsted, to developing practice that meets those requirements. Children's play and learning are often tightly harnessed, putting play on the agenda, with teachers involved in capturing opportunities to interpret and regularise moments of development and learning in order to account for it in artificially described curriculum terms. In this way, teaching and learning become 'tidy' and learning accounts can easily record progress in 'subjects'. The apparent requirement for teachers to perform in this way has been extensively discussed earlier, in Chapter 3. However, in Janette's and Matthew's classrooms, their tasks are much more complex as they recognise that children are themselves both instructor and learner and that teaching and learning often have different rhythms.

The children in their care

The ways in which Janette and Matthew discuss individual children in their care demonstrate the knowledge and understanding they have of them, developed from close observations of individuals and conversations held, over time and in a range of different circumstances. This level of intimate knowledge of the children informs each encounter as well as their plans for opportunities and experience. In the following extract Matthew carefully describes and deconstructs a shared play activity and reveals his detailed knowledge of his co-player, as well as his trust in the planned play context in his classroom:

> [She] looked and noticed that her hand had made a print on there and she looked at it and looked at me and said 'handprint', and so I did it and M, who was playing alongside, did it as well, and that led to some very giggly hand print making, and look what you can do when the sand is wet. K was very excited by the hand printing, so she does actually, now that I'm thinking about it, very, very often likes to do things on her hand – we were just painting on the wall the other day, and she was the only one to start painting on her hand, printing on her hand; whenever the paint is out, she's very into hand-type things ... I wouldn't plan necessarily to do anything with that, the opportunities are there whenever she needs to do that, do the hand things she does, because there are enough opportunities to do something messy, or cooking, or there's enough for her to initiate things and for her to get enough out of that, I don't think I have to take that anywhere.

From this kind of observational knowledge of an individual child, Matthew is able to consider her learning and resourcing needs and the level of interaction that adults need to provide to 'help' K to achieve her intentions. Matthew trusts children to learn with the level of help that he provides.

Janette talked about the way that she could see that what she was offering to the children sometimes connected with them:

> Like on the carpet, and D, and you can see in his eyes that this is what he needs and what he wants, can't you, you can see by the look on his face, whereas for other children it wasn't what they needed at that time, so they've chosen something else; but you can tell I'm getting it right just for this minute. Maybe I'll lose it and it'll come back but this is right for D.

Noticing children in this way is a particular feature of the practice of both teachers. They notice the children as people with individual characteristics, likes and dislikes, as well as young learners with particular learning needs. Having noticed them, their teachers can then feed the children's intentions in ways that will help them. Although this sounds rather simple and straightforward, it is not. This kind of teaching is highly complex and requires knowledgeable teachers and subtle interactions.

Families and communities

Although at the beginning of the project Matthew was working in a relatively affluent area, with children who in general were evidently well cared for and supported, by the end of the period of study both Matthew and Janette were teaching in areas of quite acute deprivation, evident in terms of standards of economic well-being and housing.

Both teachers expressed the view that working with children includes working with families and carers. They demonstrate respect for the children's families and communities in their descriptions and in their practice. When discussing his practice, Matthew is clear that 'we're all in this together', his conviction that strong relationships are at the forefront of good practice includes relationships with those related to the children: siblings, parents and carers. He wants parents to feel that they are also part of the learning process and to know that he values them. Janette had decided that 'only by understanding and responding to parents, supporting them, will I have any lasting impact on the child'. She continued, 'If the family's struggled and continues to struggle, then what are we [nursery workers] doing about it?' In Janette's nursery, parents are welcome to settle their children, to take time, to stay for as much of the session that they want to; their name is added to the 'adults present' list and they are included incidentally in songs, games and play.

Matthew is concerned, as mentioned earlier in relation to multiple narrative layers, in the way that his name was used by the children and their families. He wants to be addressed as Matthew although the children called him Mr Matthew. At first, many of the parents, particularly those from African cultures, felt that using his first name was disrespectful. He has taken time to talk to those parents who were concerned and told them that respect, in his view, does not come from a name but from the relationships he builds with the children. He is finding though that, while the parents are beginning to accept his position, the rest of the Early Years staff are not prepared to join him, but insist on the Mrs/Miss in case 'children view them differently', suggesting the construction of a more distant, and perhaps power-weighted, relationship. He says that sometimes the children call him 'Miss' too and is concerned that relationships are not 'flowering' as he would hope because 'any old Miss will do' as the children are 'lumping' all staff together. Matthew likens this to calling children 'boy' or 'girl' and is convinced that 'this Miss business' is getting in the way of emotional connections. Matthew's concern over this detail of his practice typifies his approach to all aspects of his work.

He places great importance on the authenticity of the relationships he is creating with the children and their families and talks about 'proper relationships', avoiding 'me the teacher, K the child' which he suggests is intrusive – 'then the magic stops'.

Both teachers exhibit a level of care towards families and express a sense of responsibility towards parents, '[I'm] surprised at how much you mean to parents' and Janette reports that parents often ask her if she 'likes' their child. Not only are these teachers able to tune into children but they are also able to tune into their worlds, in the knowledge that children's situations, their families and communities, influence their world-making, their development and their learning.

Government priorities, statutory requirements and the specified curriculum

The teachers are knowledgeable about central government initiatives, their statutory duties and the Foundation Stage requirements. Both frequently attend courses in their local authority on a range of topics relating to early years practice. Their practice is very carefully planned and recorded, as required; adult-directed activities take place in both nurseries, as required in the new statutory documentation (DCFS 2007) – in Matthew's nursery, it happens at the beginning of the session and in Janette's at the end of each session. In both nurseries this is a small proportion of the session, with the balance in favour of children's play. Janette and Matthew both report that the directed activities are a response to prior observations of children's activities during play – 'if we'd noticed them doing X, so it may be it's good for them to do Y'. The children are encouraged to participate but not coerced. The teachers were concerned about the emphasis on 'next steps' for children, with Janette describing the whole concept of predicting and directing next steps as 'malarkey'. While Matthew discussed with his team what the children would benefit from, he troubled with them too about the issue of 'next steps', asking 'Is it the next step and how do you know it's the next step and would that really be the next thing and perhaps they need to spend the next two weeks doing exactly the same thing?' Both teachers were concerned that children could be forced through a programme rather than having opportunities to repeat, rehearse or revisit the same activities frequently if they chose to do so, for their own reasons. They are, however, very rigorous about monitoring and recording children's activities and achievements, 'learning journeys' in Janette's nursery, and these could be social achievements as well as progression in the conventional cognitive sense. Matthew is clear that 'having high expectations of [children] and wanting them to achieve as much as they possibly can and more than that' was as much as could be expected of a teacher, 'there's no right way of doing it, is there, providing you can see that things are happening'. While this may be naïvely expressed, Matthew's close attention to children, noticing and noting progress, is evidence of a teacher committed to ensuring that 'things' do indeed happen. Both teachers had recently received very favourable Ofsted reports of their practice.

Their skills

From the evidence of observations of practice, video material and the teachers' own descriptions of what they do, some of their specific teaching skills can be identified.

During the period of study Janette and Matthew demonstrated the ability to perform the following skills and to reflect upon their importance:

- listen
- play
- respond
- demonstrate respect for children
- relate and make connections
- combine many activities at the same time
- lead (both children and adults)
- model (for children and adults)
- support (both children and adults)
- apply interpersonal skills (with children and adults)
- 'do the voices' (a complex notion, further explained later in the study)
- record and assess children at play
- manage – the space, the resources, the opportunities for play, the people
- guide learning (both social and cognitive) (of both children and adults).

It is interesting to consider here that some of these skills are applied not only to their work with children but also as the leader of a team of adults who benefit from models of practice and levels of support. This is a substantial list and each of these skills was not only demonstrated, but applied with subtlety and care to detail. For example, listening to children in Janette's terms means 'If children talk, you stop and listen just as when a grown-up talks, and if they talk over you, you try very hard to say, "Excuse me, one minute, I'll talk to you in a moment," but you do go back and say, "What was that you were telling me?, I couldn't listen properly."' Listening, in Janette's terms, is a very active skill, frequently employed. It involves making eye contact, engaging with the content of talk, appreciating what is being said and responding. This level of listening takes time though, but in both teachers' practice the time spent listening to young children contributes to the pace of the day.

The most important aspect of the skills listed above is that they are all contained within the teachers' notion of 'helping' children, being of use to them in their learning.

At this point, it is worth pausing to consider the challenging notion, mentioned earlier, of Bernstein's theories of invisible pedagogies (1997). The list above could be divided into two quite different sections; that is List A: a list of skills employed to allow physical and conceptual space for children to construct their own words and worlds, and List B: a list of skills used to harness, however unintentionally, the worlds and words of children to gently form them into socially acceptable shapes that can be accounted for in contemporary conventional ways. Such categorisations can easily then demonstrate the fact that, however much they lack the intention to manipulate or to be other than neutral in their work with children and families (see Janette's comments in Chapter 6), these attributes could easily be seen as contributing to practices of social construction, the invisible pedagogy of Bernstein's theories. Indeed, Matthew's insistence that the children in his nursery were 'being reasonable, social, sociable children who are being kind and sharing and have good decent relationships with the adults and the children' is a perfect example of the ways in which his practice is shaping children.

Even 'listening' could be construed as having social meaning, as choices about what and who we choose to listen to are embedded in our own social situations, cultural understandings and notion of professional responsibilities.

If we accept that in life we cannot be neutral, we may all become 'palimpsests, tablets on which successive scripts are written' (Bryan 2004: 143) (unless we are completely reclusive, in which case, that fact too becomes part of the script). This is an involuntary process, then the 'wittingness' of both learners and teachers exists exclusively in opportunities, and the ability, to reflect upon this, conceptualise it, nourish, accept or reject aspects, that is, to employ a reflexive metacognitive approach to experience and encounter. When Janette reflected upon this (see transcript extract in Chapter 6), she spoke about knowing the Janette-ness of her work. It is my thesis that play provides this opportunity and that adults, teachers, in and around children playing are responsible for knowing and understanding their role in this, that is, being completely clear that we are all culturally shaped and cultural shapers. I believe that Matthew's claim that he is helping the children in his care to develop 'decent' relationships is made 'wittingly', without defence of what he may mean by 'decent'. To engage at this level, to incorporate knowingly and reflectively what may be described as the sub-skills listed above, is a key skill of the two teachers in the study.

Knowledgeable and skilful practice

What I am claiming then is that the currently highly influential work of those educationalists and others who claim the play space in educational settings (see, for example, Siraj-Blatchford 2004), offers only a very limited, reductionist view of what is possible. Headlines drawn from such research, as discussed earlier, essentially become diluted for popular consumption. Importantly, then, the kind of messages given has the potential to damage children's opportunities in life rather than enhance them, treating children as 'amorphous blobs' (Gopnik *et al.* 1999: 152) rather than celebrating them as the brain-builders and self-makers that we are learning that children can be. The extract chosen below, and cited earlier in this study, is symptomatic of the appropriation of play:

> The provision of exploratory play environments (e.g. sand/water play) will only be *'effective'* if the materials/apparatus are *chosen carefully to provide cognitive challenge* within the *zone of proximal development and positive outcomes* for the activity are either modelled, demonstrated, explained or otherwise *identified* in the children's experiences and actions, *and encouraged.*
>
> (Siraj-Blatchford and Sylva 2004: 727, my italics)

I have italicised some of the vocabulary in this statement that provides specific clues to a preordained purpose, an agenda, for children's play here. The term 'effective' is used frequently now in all works on education, although its meaning is rarely exposed. A series of questions must be asked of this text, for example:

1 In whose terms can play be described as 'effective'?
2 Are the cognitive challenges chosen in relation to normative references, that is, stage or age theories of learning?
3 Who defines the 'zone of proximal development' and decides what is 'positive' and may not be?
4 In whose terms are these identified and then encouraged?
5 When was a consensus sought and found on the above?

An alternative view to that expressed above is often crudely characterised in over-simplistic terms, such as in this comment:

> Some ... might consider, for example, that it would be enough to support children in developing their individuality and self-expression ... Such a view may even be seen as supported by popular notions of the 'kindergarten' where children may be seen as developing naturally and requiring minimal nurture.
>
> (Siraj-Blatchford 2004: 138)

It is in this way, by patronising and diminishing alternative views, that 'popular notions' of quality are then shaped towards what is often regarded as common sense and therefore non-negotiable (see Pring's discussion of Truth, Knowledge and Power, 2004: 218–20). This kind of view, offered above, is sometimes described as 'folk theory', describing a 'folk pedagogy' (Desforges 2000: 25) that may not be visible or exist in life. Certainly, in the reflections and practice of the two teachers in my study, there is no evidence of any thinking that anything may be 'enough', which would suggest satisfaction with an adequacy rather than striving, as Matthew claimed, for the very best that children can achieve, and more.

In my study, the role of two rather remarkable teachers has been found to fit neither of the models suggested above. They do not appropriate play for spurious reasons of so-called 'effectiveness' nor do they leave children alone to develop naturally. They engage in proactive, reflexive practice while creating and responding to multiple narrative layers in their professional lives. In my study, through narrativising their experience, the teachers were able to define aspects of their identity, their influences and their practices. While their conversations and responses ranged across a wealth of issues, a critical appraisal of their work and understandings can be collected under four main headings: (1) mentors and inspirations; (2) words and talk; (3) play and players; and (4) reflection and metacognition. From this, some conclusions and implications may be drawn.

Mentors and inspirations

The practices described in this study are unusual and inspirational to observe. As in any practice, we talk of building our work on the shoulders of those who have gone before us, the giants in our field, so too the practice of the teachers in this study has been grown and cultivated from rich sources. Both teachers naturally acknowledge their parents and families as the prime influence in relation to the development of their values and their sense of self. However, Janette's response went further and acknowledged at a deep level of conviction how her father has been a model for her behaviour and respect for children from babyhood and infancy through their childhood, 'That's the way my dad talks to my children now, the way I talk to children, I suppose … genuinely interested and genuinely valuing of them and treating them as a full person.'

Both teachers also spoke enthusiastically about early career mentors, colleagues and head teachers or managers. At an early and therefore an influential point in their careers, Janette and Matthew discussed the professional community in which they found themselves and about individual people with whom they could connect in a personal way. Janette talked about the way that the teachers in her first school all worked together to prepare materials, 'thinking through', being organised and talking together. Matthew described an early mentor, a teacher who he felt was 'like' him; she read the same newspapers, enjoyed the same things. And from these colleagues, both teachers considered how they appropriated elements of their practice; Matthew thought 'yes, I'd like to be like you' and talked about shared values.

'Respect' is an attribute that they both appeared to value in those they had met. Janette described an early manager as saying that staff must only work for the children's convenience and not for their own, and now this respectful work ethic is carried into her own leadership of colleagues. Matthew enthused about his first headteacher's positive and enthusiastic approach and how he felt that was infectious. He liked the way that she always made time for him, to find something in his room and with the children to be positive about, acknowledging that 'she was quite inspirational really'.

Rather than such interpersonal influences creating a script for these young teachers, inscribing practice, palimpsest-like, Janette and Matthew seemed simply to connect with other people who held similar values, whose constructions of children were similar and whom they felt in tune with in a personal way. This confirmed their own views and consolidated their ideas about working with children. Janette, rather inspirationally herself, remembered *Equus*, a play she had seen by Peter Shaafer, in which the main character of a psychiatrist is attempting to explain the disturbed behaviour of a young boy who has exhibited extreme behaviour. She says,

> There's a quote ... about the moments snapping together. Why do some moments of experience snap together? He's trying to explain the lad's behaviour in the play, which is what you're asking, isn't it? Where do those behaviours come from, and in one of those he's asking why the moments snap together.

Interestingly, this is a play that I had seen in one of its first performance in 1973 as a young undergraduate student and there is a fascinating analogous connection to be made, although Janette herself does not explicitly make it here. The psychiatrist in the play is torn with self-doubt in his critical analysis of his role and of himself, claiming that his job has been to make children 'normal' but in doing so he is 'cutting out' their individuality. The actual quotation that Janette is remembering is this:

> A child is born into a world of phenomena all equal in their power to enslave. It sniffs – it sucks – it strokes its eyes over the whole uncomfortable range. Suddenly it strikes. Why? Moments snap together like magnets, forging a chain of shackles. Why? I can trace them. I can even, with time, pull them apart again. But why at the start they were ever magnetized at all – just those particular moments of experience and no others – I don't know. *And nor does anyone else.*
>
> (Shaffer 1973: 74; italics in original)

Janette's unprompted memory of this moment in the play is coincidental in a way, but it demonstrates her thoughtful interpretations and her own metacognitive striving in our research conversations. The quotation represents clearly the problems that she herself was grappling with, how to explain the connectedness of experience and the ways that our values drive us towards experiences, and people, that go on to matter to us in our developing lives; the tensions involved in the potential to 'enslave' children. With the influence of her father's strong relationships with her own children in mind, with his personal values and lifestyle choices in mind, Janette and Matthew would invariable connect with like-minded people in their professional lives. This is also interesting in relation to our own research relationships.

And so, in the first years of their careers, Janette and Matthew forged relationships with other professionals who *helped* to shape their practice. They found themselves working with people whom they respected and from whom they learned key lessons that would stay with them through their professional lives. Would it have been possible for Janette and Matthew to have worked in a different way with children, if they had not had these significant encounters at a stage when they were open to ideas? Matthew believes that his practice reflects his personality, 'the way I like to do it, the way I like to be'. Perhaps they met the kind of people they had because of the people they are. Nevertheless, they were drawn, for whatever reason, towards people and pedagogies that enabled them to work now in 'the plane of the personal'. Nias describes this as the way in which teachers look for 'a sense of "fit" between their self image, their place of work and what the work itself involves ... a harmony between their substantial selves and the social context of their work' (1989: 44), and this certainly makes sense in view of the teachers' earlier comments.

Both teachers also discussed the influence of their own children and how reflecting upon their strengths and challenges was helping them to consider the children in their care in their nurseries. These kinds of family observational opportunities caused them to reflect on their roles as parents and as teachers, particularly during play, as well as the ways that their children were learning and the ways that they seemed to be 'teaching' themselves. Invariably, with children at, or close to, the stage at which they were working, strategies and observations will cross over from home to school and in the other direction.

Words and talk

Both Piaget's (1959) and Vygotsky's (1978, 1986) works in relation to talk are complex but seminal; they created the possibility for many colleagues and disciples to follow, and are therefore central to any discussion of young children's development and play and adults' roles in this. Their research understanding of the dialogic nature of learning helps to critically appraise the nature of the encounters between children and the two teachers in this study. Although Piaget's conclusions suggest that the development of language moves from egocentric speech towards socialised speech and Vygotsky's appear to be the reverse, from social constructions towards inner speech, both in fact signify the importance of young children's talk during play. Piaget's extension of the notion of monologue to include 'dual or collective monologues'

(1959: 9), describes exactly the ways that children cursorily acknowledge the presence of others in the action of play but do not necessarily expect them to actively contribute or understand.

In settings where a storying play pedagogy is evident, as in this study, children and children and children and their teachers frequently participate in talk encounters in this way, seemingly to each other without necessarily expecting a reply. Their talk behaviours appear intuitive and are contained within trusting relationships. Neither the teachers nor the children appear to have preordained outcomes in mind in this level of serious play. In a way similar to Shotter's notion of 'joint action' (1993: 4), Piaget describes how, during such dual or collective monologues, 'words thrown out are caught on the bounce, like balls' (Piaget 1959: 13). Janette personifies this in her responses to what I described as a surreal talk encounter transcribed earlier. Janette reifies this kind of adult talk behaviour, claiming that 'it is not enough to be a presence or a sounding board'. So then, what is her role, or Matthew's, as they catch words from the children 'on the bounce'? When they each defined their roles, particularly in play, Janette claimed that 'it's about being someone very important, being close', and Matthew said that 'the greatest thing that I do now is just being another person there but a grown-up person'. From the significance of 'closeness', however, both teachers moved to much more closely defining their behaviour, their talk behaviours in detail and these were categorised in Chapter 6. Vološinov takes this role in talk to a different metaphorical level, suggesting that 'a word is a bridge thrown between myself and another' (1973: 86). In play, the word can be a bridge of many parts, fulfilling different functions that may meet children's social, emotional or momentary cognitive needs; helping children to define themselves by who and what they are connecting with, how and in what context. These kinds of dialogic exchanges in play cannot be predetermined but are creative and responsive. Instead, as Shotter describes, we do not 'act solely "out of" our own "inner scripts", "plans", or "ideas", but must be sensitive in some way to the opportunities and barriers, the enablements and constraints, "afforded" to us' (1993: 6). Such affordances and sensitivity to the moment should not be confused with opportunism, snatching at children's talk in order to reshape it, but is instead more subtle as the teachers' attendance in play offers affordances to co-construct the 'bridge'. The solid foundations of such a bridge, the principled understandings of the teachers, enable connections to be made, 'if one end of the bridge depends on me, then the other depends on my addressee' (Volosinov 1973: 86). It is in this detail, in the detail of responses, that teacherly skills are really visible.

Discourse, talk and word, cannot be separated though from those who engage with it. While Matthew is clear that a significant aspect of his work with children is in encouraging 'good, decent relationships' between the children and between adults and children, it is *his* notion of 'good' and 'decent' that is being encouraged, as previously discussed. Bakhtin claims, 'it is not out of a dictionary that the speaker gets his words, but rather it exists in other people's mouths' (1981: 294). From Matthew, then, the children in his care will learn ideas of 'goodness' and 'decency' and these children's 'ideological becoming' develops in 'the process of selectively assimilating the words of others' (ibid.: 341). Such assimilation appears inescapable, worthy of consideration but not necessarily negative in any sense, and, as in Matthew's case, may be a force for positive social outcomes, wittingly conceived. This example of 'invisible pedagogy' is included here for acknowledgement, though it is not the centre of this section.

Talk, then, is a key feature in the practice of the two teachers studied. It is allowed to proliferate, and the responses given exist on a continuum ranging from addressivity to mediation of concepts, meanings and action. Both teachers are ready to acknowledge the socio-cultural nature of learning in their support for talk in their practice. While this may be true for many teachers, those in this study applied their understandings of how children are best supported by significantly respecting children's intentionality. The children themselves directed the bridge building of the word, referred to earlier; the children initiated, led and invariably ended conversations and narrative co-constructions; and it was the self-initiated, self-directed, play action of the children that fed talk exchanges. In these nurseries, play contexts form the bedrock on which the dialogic exchanges exist, 'grounded in the extralinguistic context of the here and now' (Karmiloff and Karmiloff-Smith 2001: 156). Janette and Matthew are helping children to learn positive attitudes towards language, encouraging turn-taking in conversation, demonstrating active listening, supporting a developing vocabulary and sustaining language exchanges, as well as providing content responses.

While the surprise of finding that their talk behaviours were differently manifested in their practice, with Janette's emphasis intuitively on narrations and Matthew's on addressivity, this has now become only a matter of emphasis, dependent on personality, rather than a factor of deeper significance. However, they are both also doing more, acting in ways that are significantly extra to the already long list of positive support. They are actively encouraging narrative constructions, through which an individual's (the child's) sense of self develops and grows (Bruner 1986; Rosen 1988; Karmiloff and Karmiloff-Smith 2001). Such constructions though, in these teachers' practices, are borne out of the children's interests, at the point of their interest, using self-appointed resources. The significance of this is that as children grow, they are undertaking a complex journey comprising intertwined processes of self-making and linguistic competence. And 'selfhood is profoundly relational' and the 'construction of selfhood cannot proceed without a capacity to narrate' (Bruner 2002: 86). It is these narrations that are being modelled, enacted and fostered so carefully in both nurseries.

How these journeys, and the construction of selfhood in children in their care, are viewed, accompanied and mediated depend solely on the skill of the adults they meet on their way. Meeting with either Janette or Matthew ensures that the spaces between early monologues or soliloquies (Piaget 1959) and the highly complex narrativisation of experience (Bruner 1986) that happen in play are supported, and supported sensitively and well. The narrativisation of experience, happening frequently in the storying events in the play of young children enables the players to 'subjunctivise reality' and engage in the 'trafficking of human possibilities, rather than in settled certainties' (Bruner 1986: 26). It seems only to be unusual adults who can escape the certainties of their own experience, 'learning to live with not knowing' (Moyles 2005a: 9) and to claim the rather riskier space of possibilities in play, as Matthew so clearly demonstrates in his narrations and in his practice.

Play and players

In both nurseries, play was assumed rather than described or justified. There were no special corners for play, time for play, or play resources. If, as the Qualifications and Curriculum Authority attempted to claim in 2000, there should be no distinction between play and work for children (QCA 2000: 11), then the classrooms of both teachers could either be described as complete workspaces or complete play sites. Children were able to choose what they did, how they performed, with what, with whom and for how long, for most of their time there. Boundaries existed in relation to anti-social play, that is any activities that interfered with other children's freedoms or that hurt or damaged children or property. However, in both nursery settings it was rare to see children being stopped in an activity, admonished or 'disciplined'. As Matthew said, 'They [the children] don't see the need to do things that people might see as misbehaving, there are too many other things to do, you know, why would I, there are other more exciting things to do than that.' What was visible was that the children became the 'play leaders' and the adults' role was complex, to both track and to understand. The teachers followed the children in their play and often played alongside.

Play is generally understood to be a complex activity; however, the difficulty in the context of my study is in deconstructing the adults' role in play, particularly their interactions. The Bakhtinian notion of 'voicing' (Bakhtin 1981) has been helpful here. In the glossary of terms to support the translation of Bakhtin's work, 'voice' is defined as 'the speaking personality, the speaking consciousness. A voice always has a will or desire behind it, its own timbre and overtones' (ibid.: 434) and in Bakhtin's work relating to the dialogic process, he also defines 'double-voiced discourse', subversions and the 'carnivalesque' nature of some dialogic functions. In Carter's discussion of these ideas, he refers to 'multivoicing' (2004: 68) and the interplay between voices, particularly in children's play. In children's storying, multivoicing can be visible and therefore easily understood, as children, generally, readily suspend reality, take on roles and develop characterisation. As Carter says in relation to learners, they are moving from the cultural context of the classroom to another (target) culture in search of what he describes as 'the third place' (sometimes defined as the imagination) in between, where 'a transformed identity' is formed. It seems then, that in the nurseries of Janette and Matthew, their multivoicing is supporting children in occupying Carter's 'third place'. Their 'voices' appear to include that of the following:

1   narrator of the play;
2   voices within play;
3   the addressee;
4   their personal voice born from their own lived lives;
5   their professional voice which represents the culture of the school and that of a public servant with statutory responsibilities.

These five voices interact with the children's and with each other, creating a 'polyphony' of voices (Wertsch 1991: 64). What is then 'heard' by the child, the learner, is what s/he appropriates and transforms in her/his narrative constructions. Words, as Bakhtin says, are 'half-ours and half-someone else's' (1981: 344) and, further, 'the ideological becoming of a human being is the process of selectively assimilating the words of others' (ibid.: 341). The significance of the adult in play is becoming magnified by these claims and they serve to justify such close scrutiny of teachers and their intentions in playing with children. Bakhtin's question 'Who precisely is speaking?' (ibid.: 340) can be set to try to deconstruct and understand the nature of the voices applied by the teachers and contained within the discourse of play.

As the children in the nurseries assimilate, 'interanimate', appropriate and negotiate language use and linguistic devices in play, play becomes a distinctive site for learning, a metacognitive context; that is children are not only active, using language, but also developing a sense of their acts and their language, as mediated by Janette and Matthew. The simple answer to the Bakhtinian question, of who is doing the talking, is that the children are, in Janette and Matthew's settings; they have control and leadership of play. The more complex answer, however, would be that there is a melding of voices, socially constructed, mediated and transformed. It is in this way that Wertsch's notion that 'mind exists beyond the skin' can be understood. This will be further explored in the concluding section.

Reflection and metacognition

It is in the reflexive nature of the two teachers' professional approaches, however, that the true value of their professionalism and their practice seems to exist. The significance of 'talk' and of 'play' as distinctive features of this practice rests in the teachers' abilities to value, reflect upon and understand intentionality, narrative constructions and voice.

Children develop metacognition in their early years, needing to act on the world but, with the development of language, also needing to know what their actions mean. It is important to remember that very young children are not passive learners but are busy and active in constructing themselves and their sense of their world, as it appears to them in their early years of life and learning. Research from other disciplines, as acknowledged earlier, is teaching educators some crucial lessons, about the activities of developing brains: 'A key aspect of our developmental picture is that babies are actively engaged in looking for patterns in what is going on around them, in testing hypothesis and in seeking explanations' (Gopnik et al. 1999: 152). The philosophical nature of young children's questioning demonstrates exactly this early ability to reason and make sense of the many worlds and experiences that are opening up to them. However, they learn very quickly to suppress their own early developing theories about learning and, in general, children very quickly adopt new learned behaviours and develop a willingness to comply. So school learning becomes a new cultural learning; children learn the culture of the school and all that implies, including embedded notions of what it means to be a child and a learner and also to value the superficial layers that may serve limited purposes but effect rewards.

An alternative to this approach has been offered to the world of education by Reggio Emilia. Their approach to working with young children has been labelled 'a pedagogy of relationships and listening', which requires teachers to engage in improvisation in their responses to children and to develop skills of 're-cognition', a process involving close observation and understanding of children's behaviour, talk and actions by their teachers (Rinaldi 2005: 19). In Reggio Emilia, the process of re-cognition takes place through documentation activities to enable ephemeral material to become tangible, invisible thinking to become visible, through the act of interpretation by the teachers.

The work of the teachers in this study is very close to the Reggio Emilia approach, allowing children sufficient time, space, resources and 'help' to both act and to reflect upon their acts, which involves both adults and children in metacognition. Intellectualising play, understanding the words and worlds that children employ in their story narratives and accounting for it in professional dialogues, creating a discourse to legitimise children's intentions and activities, are the work of very skilled practitioners. In order to fulfil their professional and statutory responsibilities, they must be confident in this level of narrative construction, as well as in the story narratives of the children and the everyday 'insider' professional narratives constructed with families and colleagues. Insider narratives involve conversations with and about children for the purposes of helping children and would include consistent questioning, such as: What are the children doing?, What do they know?, What are they demonstrating that they know?, What then do they need?, What am I doing and why?, What else could I do?, What do I know about this content?, How can I help? Embedded in the kind of practice that

Janette and Matthew encompass is the deep understanding that knowledge and learning are processed 'between people (interpsychological) and then inside (the child) (intrapsychological) (Vygotsky 1978: 57). This applies not only to the children but also, in articulating their understanding of the children and their development and their learning, a kind of oral documentation (Rinaldi 2005) is taking place with the teachers as they apply a metalanguage to their engagements in play. As Matthew said, 'I think about what I do a lot and why I do it and I think about the children a lot, what they're doing and why they do it and how I can support them to do it, what they might need to help them get to where they might want to go.' Janette was clear too about how she understood moments of learning with children:

> You can see it in his eyes, a connection and a ha, ha moment ... when you're meeting the child's needs, you're meeting your own need to have the child's needs met; that's your need as a teacher, isn't it, your professional need ... from that comes a reciprocal relationship perhaps. That's rewarding in itself, isn't it?

In the same way that children engage in self-making through their reflective play acts, so too do teachers in their explorations of their own roles, their engagements and their deconstructions of children's learning because 'self rises out of our capacity to reflect upon our own acts, by the operation of metacognition' (Bruner 1986: 67). There are clear implications here for the kinds of opportunities used in this research project to be replicated in and between networks of practice, where trusting relationships can be formed to support such engagement.

Chapter 8

Conclusion
Mind and body, values and action

In my research project I have sought close collaboration with colleagues, two teachers, in order to understand and reflect upon their work and their influences. This has been achieved through the construction of narratives of experience. I have carefully considered the process of gathering data and the tensions in finding ways of analysing, reporting, and reflecting upon it, a process which has itself been interesting. I believe, as Desforges claims, that 'if we can advance our understanding of intersubjective exchange we would enhance our pedagogic capacity by a quantum leap and massively extend our abilities to teach through a 'pedagogy of mutuality' (Desforges 2000: 26).

My contention in this research has been to evidence this, not only in the work of the two teachers chosen to represent and narrate such a pedagogic approach, but also in my own research practices. My intentions in the project have been to collect insider information and reflections, to translate this into outsider interpretations and to represent this for analysis.

In this project, as researcher, I have tried to embody principles of encounter described above, by collaborating with teachers with whom it was possible to work because of trusting reciprocal relationships, developed over time and in a range of contexts. I wanted to give them time to talk, to reflect and to narrate their values and their practice. This is, however, a process and not an event and I have consistently worried about damaging relationships and asking too much of them. It may be that my outsider self was not sufficiently detached from the work as I was, and remain, in awe of their practice and of their ability to engage in critical reflection of their values, their professional lives and their own narrations. However, by acknowledging this from the beginning and throughout the report I have claimed 'authoritative knowledge' as well as recognising 'the ideology which is embedded in [my] own discourse, methods and theories' (Holliday 2002: 15). Holliday also discusses the ways that qualitative researchers 'spin ways of talking about reality' (ibid.: 15) and in my research project such spinning rests upon the relationship with my two colleagues and is based securely on my knowledge of their abilities to reflect themselves and their work in narratives of experience. At the end of what may have been a gruelling period of self-reflection for them, I believe the relationships to have remained intact. This way of working, as a relational researcher, was, I believe, a 'best fit' for me, although clearly there are lessons to be learned and some challenging ideas to pursue further.

There are also implications for future projects in relation to the tools employed and, in particular, examining the use of video material may repay further consideration. Film is a seductive media and, while I acknowledge its worth and the use of teachers' own material, it became evident very quickly that these two teachers were, in many ways, beyond the level of simply interpreting film or even requiring it as a prompt. While both talked of finding the material 'interesting' (and they were indeed of high quality in content terms), they were much more motivated towards deep conversations of meaning and motive. Once they had both 'confirmed' through the video material that they were operating in familiar (if not identical) roles and patterns of behaviour, that in itself became sufficient to provide permission to safely range over the issues detailed earlier. The film then became the evidence that all three of us required to ensure that we shared the same language in our conversations about play, play pedagogies and play spaces. Rather than dig deeper into the play episodes themselves (although an interesting project to carry out with a more random sample, see Adams 2005: 213–27), my project became a study outside of that, concerned centrally with the people themselves and their narrations. Although they became almost a distraction in our research conversations, the video materials were fascinating for me to view and they helped in establishing themes and threads throughout.

Teaching has been described as an art by Piaget (1959) and there is more to uncover and present in relation to teachers as artists in early years practice but also through all educational phases. This links to another very significant and closely connected area of interest, which is to pursue the art of conversation, 'common talk' (Carter 2004), in classrooms and between children and children and their teachers, to identify how this may help children in making connections between elements of their everyday lives. Conversations were a central feature of this project, invaluable, informal and revealing and I also believe them to be contexts of creativity, at all levels.

Towards a distinctive definition of practice

A coat
I made my song a coat
Covered with embroideries
Out of old mythologies
From heel to throat;
But the fools caught it,
Wore it in the world's eyes
As though they'd wrought it.

Song, let them take it,
For there's more enterprise
In walking naked.

(Yeats 1994)

This poem has assumed significance in relation to play. Metacognition is briefly discussed below but, play as a metacognitive context may re-clothe this slippery business of teaching and learning into a new multi-woven embroidered coat, attractive to many interests. I believe that the two teachers in this study are operating in a very different way from many of their colleagues. This has been evidenced in my own professional and personal experience, although more sustained research is a clear implication of my study. However, the teachers in this research collaboration are able to clearly articulate their intentions, their values and their strong commitment towards children and their families. Some conclusions can be drawn about their practice and principles and much of it centres on their strong faith in children as learners and in their trust in the context of play.

Currently, in England, much is being made of play; as a term it is being variously defined, variously interpreted, appropriated and used to label and market a range of products, resources, activities and schemes. Perhaps the activities in which these two teachers engage may be better left 'naked' without title rather than occupying the same space as other more didactically managed activities in early years settings. However, if it is possible to persist with Bruce's definitive and unequivocal statement that one of the key founding principles of play, is that 'children choose to play, they cannot be made to play' (2005: 132) then the way that play is 'worn' cannot be mistaken.

At the conclusion of this study, there are eight distinct elements that define the practice of the two teachers who participated in the research and which make them distinctive and, in my terms, remarkable. With the benefit of this list of attributes, drawn from the evidence in the narratives of my two teachers and discussed below, it may become rather more possible to define 'teaching' for the early years of education, at least, and to develop some thoughts about appropriate pedagogies, which is another term worthy of deconstruction.

Throughout this work, as in any academic study, there have been problems of language and vocabulary. For example, the way now that 'learning' is consistently harnessed to 'curriculum' in many policy documents and texts as if the two are bound together, and, more visibly, the way that 'teaching' is often used synonymously with 'instruction'. Language of course carries meaning with it and layers of cultural understandings. If clear policy and consensual policies are to be sought, then defining terms is an inescapable task to be confronted at the earliest opportunity by all of those engaged in educational debate. The alternative is that half of us will be 'walking naked'.

Defining elements of practice

1. Helping children

This is such a simple phrase and yet it is an accurate description of much of the very subtle, multi-layered activities in which Janette and Matthew engage. Their ideas about 'fitting in' with children's play and 'being of use' illustrate how trusting they are of the children to lead and to define their own terms of learning. 'Helping children get to where they might want to go' suggests a reciprocity that is unusually structured in teacher–child relationships. In this kind of relationship, power is more equally distributed and children's perceptions of themselves as being in control of action and circumstances with adults as facilitators, contributes to their growing sense of self and the ways that they feel they can act upon the world. Children can be helped, however, only if there exists a trusting relationship with their teacher, a 'genuine' relationship in Matthew's terms, which allows them to service play according to their professional understandings and their personal, intersubjective, knowledge and skills.

2. 'Wittingness' (Peters 1966: 42)

Teaching involves enormous responsibilities. Teachers are entrusted on a daily basis with children's lives and development and should therefore be in a position to articulate what it is that determines their actions, behaviour and attitudes to children, childhood and learning. It is an important finding of this study that both teachers were clearly conscious of their actions, language and behaviour as they themselves 'acted on' the play contexts of children. Their ideas about helping children and their deep knowledge of individual children enabled them to act intentionally in every aspect of their work. Their subsequent ability to articulate these actions as fluently as they have is a testament to their professionalism. Incidental learning does not happen as a result of incidental teaching but rather as a consequence of the planned environments, resources, interactions and adult interventions that 'witting' teachers have carefully designed.

3. Respect of intentionality

In this study, the teachers demonstrated trust in children as learners. Further, they were able to respect that 'in play children are a head taller than themselves' (Vygotsky 1978: 102) and that creativity in young children is boundless. Listening to children is a skill that is often underdeveloped and underused although if genuinely playing with children, then it must grow in teachers to become highly sensitised as their intentions are sometimes initially hard to discern. Invariably, however, young children's actions precede or accompany words and the act of the 'squidgelling' child in Janette's setting would be hard to ignore. The immense challenge for teachers of young children who play, however, is to be able to account for children's learning and their development without children necessarily being aware of that layer of professional activity. In this way, children's intentions in play can be honoured without fear of compromise and the secondary business of making connections to broad national standards and formalising the children's achievements becomes an adult-only activity, an out-of-contact task, an additional narrative layer.

4. Encouraging narrative constructions

Understanding storying play contexts was the original focal point of this research project. Stories at all levels are evidently important in both nurseries. The teachers read and told stories. They constructed stories with, alongside, and about the children. Fantasy, paradoxically, became a fact of life in both nurseries. The small piece of oral text quoted in Chapter 6, relating to fish needing spoons to eat yoghurt and mermaids existing in cupboards, was an incidental exchange occupying only a few moments of time but nevertheless really illustrating the idea that reality could be readily suspended and *anybody* had the power to decide what was real. And so a Tardis could be made from blocks in the playground, rockets could fly to school, dinosaurs slept under the sand but lived in houses and anybody could be a prince or a princess for the day. Everybody engaged in narrative constructions. Everyone was a storyteller.

5. Inhabiting risky spaces in play

In Matthew's nursery he was happy to find out *with* the children what would happen in any context. He felt safe not knowing. This is a risky space for teachers to occupy and requires a level of confidence in the play space created, in children and in learning possibilities as well as children's own ability to cope with uncertainty. Shotter describes such a place as 'a zone of uncertainty' (1999: 4) where we may act spontaneously, contingently and responsively. These kinds of spaces are creative and often inspirational, leading to huge rafts of possibilities from which children could develop their play. Matthew was as safe in his co-constructions in the sand tray as he was next to the physically rather risky and very tall Tardis construction from large blocks that a group of children had made. He was prepared to wait for them to realise that the tower needed support and a broader base on which to balance, which they did through conversation and their own developing sense of logic.

6. Valuing play as a distinctive site for learning

In both nurseries, play was assumed rather than planned or predicted. That is, the settings were both unquestionably play sites. Equally, in both nurseries, the teachers were giving value to play by playing with children rather than occupying the more traditional roles of engaging in instructional acts, pencil and paper activities that are generally curriculum subject-related and objectives-driven. They modelled this alternative behaviour for the rest of their nursery teams and all adults 'played', giving unspoken status to play. Play did not appear at any time to be separated out from other activities. That is, there was no distinction between 'play' and 'work'. Very brief spells of teacher-led activities took place, often involving songs or games or recall and invariably including play*fulness*. Observations and records were sometimes made of children while they were playing and these formed the basis for the later constructed 'learning logs', 'learning journeys' or records of assessment which fed into the children's Early Years Profile.

7. Play as a metacognitive process

It is noticeable that, as the children were playing in the nurseries, they were also helped to understand their play, either in Janette's distinctive style of play narration or in Matthew's rather more reticent style as addressee and facilitator. As children played and acted on the world, they were encouraged to also narrate and make sense of their own activities. Talk as the central focus enabled this level of metacognition to take place. As discussed earlier, Rinaldi talks of re-cognition (2005: 23) and this term is helpful in understanding the ways that children re-narrate their understanding as it develops, storying their way through the day, making connections and having those connections supported and reinforced by mediating adults. However, as Matthew rightly said, relationships are everything and they must be trusting relationships between those adults and individual children.

8. Melding of voices, socially constructed, mediated and transformed

In both nurseries, it was not clear at times who led the stories, who created them, defined the action or transformed it. The sounds that could be heard were of the joint actions of children and adults together, resolving conflict at the sand tray, deciding about midnight feasts and sleepovers or constructing pathways for dinosaurs. Adults and children were 'multivoicing'; on one level, they were constructing the basic story narrative together, on another, they were 'doing the voices' in the story, on another, they were directing the play according to the socially constructed narrative of home and/or experiences. In addition, the teachers were controlling the adult narrative of pedagogic practice, retaining the narrative of monitoring and assessment and sometimes supplying vocabulary. Adults and children were both insiders and outsiders to the play action, inside and outside of reality and fantasy. 'Voices' representing the consciousness of individuals became melded in these circumstances until the origins became lost in the richness of the event and support became invisible.

Conclusion and implications

During a conference address, Wertsch gave an everyday example of how his idea that the 'mind extends beyond the skin' might work in life. He talked of the way that a child may have lost his Wellington boots. She would ask the adult, 'Where are my boots?' The adult may reply with another question, for example, 'Where did you have them last?' and together a reconstruction, a 're-cognition' perhaps in Rinaldi's terms, would occur until the boots were to be found through the joint action between adult and child (Wertsch 2007). There is a deeper level to be reached in understanding Wertsch's image of the 'mind extending beyond the skin' and the idea of the melding of voices, than in the transparent and limited way that the now rather disreputable metaphor of 'scaffolding' is applied.

In Daniels' deeply illuminating critical appraisal of Vygotsky's work and theories, he outlines ranges of 'pedagogic practice' that have developed out of Vygotsky's inspirational research work. The labels for these include 'Reciprocal Teaching', 'Cognitive Apprenticeships', 'Instructional Conversations', 'The Fifth Dimension' and 'Third Space Pedagogy' (Daniels 2007: 307–31). Models of practice are often created and discussed in this way in attempts to provide labels and to categorise work with children that does not sit comfortably in legitimised curriculum terms. And, in a challenge to the kinds of practice described as 'remarkable' in this study, it has been argued 'but if there is no legitimate curriculum to be taught in the early years then there is clearly no need for teachers/educators' (Siraj-Blatchford 2004: 138). I would argue that it is in these circumstances that the most skilled, knowledgeable and intuitive teachers are required, like Janette and Matthew, who are able to work and play with children according to their development and learning needs rather than imposing a pre-formed, apparently age-appropriate, one-size-fits-all curriculum. In attempts to make sense of teaching, school and education and to satisfy the current need for close public accountability, it certainly appears as if 'pedagogical pegs' are needed to account for the ways in which teachers teach through interactions rather than rely upon instruction and transmission.

In his celebration of Freire's revolutionary work in literacy, Giroux helps with his definition of school, claiming that 'schooling is about the regulation of time, space, textuality, experience, knowledge and power amidst conflicting interests and histories that simply cannot be pinned down in simple theories of reproduction and resistance' (1987: 14). This rather functional and dispiriting definition reflects an instrumental and expedient ideological base for the 'schooling' of children. Understanding the vocabulary is a small start to understanding the world and possibly all educational texts now need to be issued with a glossary of terms to define the ways in which language has been appropriated; terms such as schooling, education, curriculum, play, pedagogy, learning, teacher and teaching. For example, in a Glossary attached to the OECD report, cited earlier, 'pedagogy' is explained:

> In English 'pedagogy' normally means 'a teaching method' and the adjective 'pedagogic' can be interchanged with 'didactic'. In the social pedagogy tradition of the Nordic and Central European countries 'pedagogy' is an approach to young children that addresses the whole person and the pedagogical relationship is one that includes integrally care, upbringing and education.
>
> (OECD 2006: 230)

And yet the assumption is often that everyone is using the same dictionary when we use such language and that our levels of understanding equip us to engage in a discourse which has appropriated that term. However, it is, as Bakhtin reminds us, 'not out of a dictionary that the speaker gets his words but rather it exists in other people's mouths' (Bakhtin 1981: 294), as definitions and meanings are culturally shaped and bound. Out of the mouths of the teachers in this study, clear 'pedagogical relationships' are being formed and sustained, similar to the Nordic tradition described above. One implication of this seems to be that this kind of practice needs to be shared rather more publicly to be understood. It may also be more useful in training and supporting colleagues in practice if we returned to using simple language with sophisticated and subtle meanings – helping children, servicing children's play, fitting in with their intentions, helping them to get where they want to go – rather than engaging in a war of words to establish primacy in the increasingly politicised debates. In the final stages of my study I wrote to both teachers to ask them what they felt was their ultimate purpose in their work with children; what were they hoping to achieve. They each answered in their now familiar committed manner:

> Empowerment is the ultimate purpose I think, so that children believe they can do it, take a risk, have a go, be themselves, be creative, use me, not use me. The outcome I expect is I want children to feel empowered. That is it in a nutshell.
>
> (Matthew)

> What is important is that children find their place, their space or identity in the world outside their family and are comfortable and competent in it. That they get support, encouragement and affirmation of their own developing skills and understandings. It's the research and enquiry and the disposition to be a learner that I am trying to promote, I think.
>
> (Janette)

What is the value, however, of knowing that 'remarkable' teachers like this exist in the world, with such finely tuned world shaking aims, if the world retains an alternate discourse to address educational policy?

As Hall claims, 'Whilst government initiatives appear to result in a lowering of professionalism and a technicist status for teachers, the new theories of learning are calling for highly sophisticated classroom facilitation by teachers and a strong knowledge base' (2004: 117). Presented with this kind of professional dichotomy, what is a teacher to do? It has been suggested that she should metaphorically 'walk on two legs' (Dahlberg *et al.* 1999), acknowledging both sets of arguments and the dual demands on teachers. However, Hall calls for 'teacher idealism' to be rekindled (2004) as the balance may have shifted away from the celebration of this in recent years. In addition, many teachers, local authority advisors and government officials 'travel', both physically and metaphorically to look for support, although Freire warns that 'it is impossible to export or import practices or experiences' (Freire and Macedo 1987: 133).

There is, however, a growing bank of evidence to suggest that the best support for developing, supporting, nourishing and sustaining practice is in research collaborations between 'insiders' and 'outsiders', both acknowledging each other's expertise so that a genuine trusting relationship can be created to serve the needs of young children in educational settings (see, for example, Medwell *et al.* 1997; David 1999; Hall 2004). Teachers who co-join with others to deconstruct and understand their own practice, by sharing observations, knowledge, and experiences for example, may be better equipped to become effective in their re-cognition of young children's learning.

Understanding the importance of both 'encounter' and the 'wittingness' of adults and children in their choices of engagement seems to be at the core of Janette's and Matthew's analysis of their pedagogy. Practice of this kind requires an openness to learn, from children and others, and the ability to adopt a meta-language to really deconstruct what may be meant by teacher knowledge and children's learning. This may be the core of the 'documentation' practices often described in the Reggio Emilia approach (Dahlberg and Moss 2005; Rinaldi 2005). In her work on teacher professionalism and literacy practices, Bryan describes 'policy drivers' and 'prismatic headteachers' as 'reality definers' (Bryan 2004: 147). In my study, the two teachers, in an interlacing between their developing sense of professional self, their intuitive practices and their knowledge of children and the children and families in their care, themselves defined the realities of teaching and learning, remarkably. In their nurseries and in conversation, they proved to be principled players and inspirational, courageous teachers. However, one might ask why teachers would need courage in their repertoire of personal attributes? What risks are being taken?

It is important to continually remember that the principles and practices of teachers are considered in the context of high levels of curriculum and pedagogical prescription currently evident in the education system in England.

Some aspects of the life histories of these teachers and the range of political, policy, institutional, cultural and cross-national influences on the teachers' identities are being examined, at a time when teachers' roles are being increasingly seen as technical in nature and skills based in content and reduced to curriculum delivery rather than 'an engagement with other minds' (Pring 2004: 68) or 'an act of love' (Freire 1976: 38). Such a delivery model often results in practice in some early years contexts where children quickly learn to comply with teachers' and institutional requirements and to forego or compromise their urges, desires, passions or dreams in favour of completing teacher-led activities, designed to propel them through a national programme of instruction (BERA SIG 2003).

I have described the teachers in my study as exceptional early years professionals whose practice more closely resembles that described by Pring and Freire above. So, in this case what are *their* influences and *their* intentions, if not to propel children through nationally designed programmes, and how can their intuitive behaviour be deconstructed? Through conversation with me the teachers describe who they believe they are and how they view their professional roles, uncovering as they do so the respect they hold for children and childhood. In their nursery classrooms, instead of 'allowing' play or relegating it to corners of time and space, play is central and is led, directed and orchestrated by children. The adults support and maintain play rather than hijacking or redefining the purposes or the action. As the stories of the teachers began to unfold, the subtlety of their practice is demonstrated and their skills, commitment and professionalism become clearly evident.

Both teachers in this study, however, are employed in the maintained sector. While this does not protect them from scrutiny in relation to national objectives, it does offer a level of professional protection from the kinds of ambitions and mind sets that may exist in some settings in the voluntary, private and independent sectors where practice is determined by those whose livelihoods may be affected by external funders and client interest which is often in turn driven by short-term gains or Ofsted results. In these circumstances compliance is ensured by narrow definitions of the EYFS requirements. This is of course counter to the aims of the Early Years Foundation Stage which was intended to regulate practice and ensure compliance. Inevitably, without providing vast national funding to professionalise the service offered to parents of young children, a reductionist and literal interpretation of the requirements will result, however well intentioned the practitioners are. There remains therefore a huge responsibility for those involved in pre-service and in-service training and education to ensure that the highest ambitions for provision are maintained. As a minimum, this must include the need for all of those practising with babies and young children to be given opportunities to reflect on their work in the company of other professionals. In her study of quality in early childhood provision, Brown discusses the 'cultures of *outsiders* and *insiders*' (Brown 2003), claiming that the 'outsiders' often prescribe the practice for 'insiders'. In her studies, Brown regards outsiders generally as prescriptive policy-makers. Her argument is that 'if innovation for improvement is to be effective it has to be rooted in ... the ways in which the *insiders* make sense of what they do, and these do not necessarily reflect the conceptual frameworks used by *outsiders*' (ibid.). It is only in this way, by teachers coming together to make sense of what they do, that the level of sophisticated thinking apparent in the practice of the teachers in this study can be achieved.

It is readily acknowledged that since 1997 there has been significant political activity around the provision of early education and care (Alexander 2010; Pugh 2010; Owen and Haynes 2010). However, there is still an apparent lack of political understanding of the need for direct attention to be given to who is looking after the needs of the youngest children in the system and what those people are doing with them in their everyday encounters although it is clear that 'children's well being in the foundation stage and success in the primary stage are strongly linked to the quality of the practitioners who support them in their earliest years' (Alexander 2010: 490).

In summary

Where have Janette and Matthew emerged from? They have had different lives, training, experiences, mentors and jobs. They cannot be said to be of one 'kind', a template for others to follow and there are key differences in their teaching behaviour, as outlined earlier. And, indeed, they have very different personalities and are very different people. There have been suggestions that teachers are 'born' rather than 'made', or, as Janette stated earlier, 'It's about knowing how you are as a person, not necessarily with children.' It is commonly believed now, in theories of child development, that there is an 'interplay' between nature and experience rather than one or other being dominant. Perhaps then it is possible to believe also that there are such enormous rewards from the positive experiences to be enjoyed with children, if working in the style of Janette and Matthew, that a self-perpetuating influence can occur. In the Reggio Emilia tradition, Malaguzzi was adamant that teachers did not develop in isolation. He claimed that:

> The gifted teacher was not to be found, cannot be found today. The gifted teacher is shaped only by working together with children and other adults, by building together, making mistakes together, correcting, revisiting and reflecting on work that has been done.
>
> (2004: 13)

Perhaps it is this very act, of children and teachers, teachers and teachers, teachers and researchers, puzzling together in re-cognition of play and pedagogy that we will create a 'special kind of teaching, not written in books' (ibid.: 11).

Appendix

The research principles, process and methods

This book is a summary of a doctoral study. A choice was made to undertake the research in a relational way in order to reflect the relational nature of the work that was under scrutiny and to demonstrate absolute respect for the two teachers whose work was being examined.

Understanding colleagues from the inside requires 'the need to work relationally, emotionally and empathically with the people whose stories we are helping to tell' (Goodley *et al*. 2004: 166). I had asked the teachers to narrate their experiences, explore a reflexive self-awareness and to share in the analyses of that narration. Human behaviour is complex in its performance and outsider interpretation is fraught with difficulty and susceptible to prejudice and bias (Holliday 2006). In an attempt to counter this, three-way conversations also took place, enabling the teacher/researcher role to be expanded. In this way, and in trusting relationships, it became possible to uncover and articulate some elements of the teachers' depth of understanding of themselves and their professional role. This kind of collaborative interpretive analysis has become central to my work. Of course, talk about professional life may not correspond with the realities of practice and so methods included gathering field notes from observation and jointly viewing video material that the participants had created, as well as these very central, semi-structured interviews. Such mixed methods have supported the idea of collecting a mosaic of research material that the teachers could review and discuss during the process of analysis. I have collected data from semi-structured interviews, semi-structured meetings, less formal conversations, video material, and field notes.

As explained in previous chapters, some theories have already been formed in relation to the two participants studied and the value of their pedagogy: I have, after all selected them for study and described them as 'exceptional'. It has also been claimed, for example, that the teachers operate an intuitive practice and give value to storying pedagogies. However, at all stages, further information was required about the origins of such organic practice as well as influences and sources of nourishment for teachers working in this way and so questions were formed to elicit this information.

An argument for messy data

My study emerged from a desire to create an honest attempt to 'tell' the stories of teachers I have described above as 'exceptional'. The purpose of this storytelling of storying pedagogies has been to identify and elicit the essence of their work with children, ostensibly in order to categorise it for dissemination. However, as in any real-world study of real people, issues arise in deconstructing, categorising and analysing data. This is partly the result of researcher identity that is, I am also an ingredient in the research, never neutral and what I would like to choose to value and give status to is the entirety of the conversations, every golden moment. Also, the notion of 'clean' data is, at best, highly questionable. Among data collected from the teachers is inevitable evidence of 'the reflective self' in this educational enquiry (Clough 2002: 82). I would like the words of the teachers to speak for themselves, in context, and in complete, connected texts. The two teachers, who were interviewed, observed and who generously gave time to research conversations, spoke willingly and openly about their beliefs and their practice. They did so articulately, often eloquently and at times almost poetically. Transforming transcripts and notes into fairly stark abstractions in an academic text can barely do justice to the time and serious thought that they have invested in this study of their work. In most cases, their words speak for themselves and any analysis seems almost tautologous. However, this has been an academic study and conventions may not safely be avoided (Holliday 2002: 101). Equally it is not, in the end, in any sense a life history of the teachers involved and therefore wholly appropriating design from that research domain may not be proper. Also, in Wertsch's terms (2007), meaning is socially constructed and can be socially distributed. If, as he claims, 'the mind extends beyond the skin', then collaboratively through the teachers' talk and academic analysis some meanings of worth can be established. The resulting presentation of data, in many ways, has been a compromise. As the architect of this work, in the context of the politics and policies of the moment as described earlier, it is important to help the presentation of the teachers' 'selves' stand out among other professional 'structures' of the time, to give them research weight and status among other constructions of teaching, which justifies in part any academic analysis of passionately felt conversations.

As a result, then, of this tension, two forms have been chosen to present and discuss the data. Clough's ideas (2002) of presenting research stories in their raw form, to cause readers to work to forge links and to make relational connections, has not quite been replicated but instead elements of the raw conversational data are provided, interwoven with discursive commentary.

Research approach

Qualitative research that claims to be an attempt to understand teachers and teaching suggests that there will not be a simple statistical or causal project to be undertaken and narrated. 'Understanding' suggests the possibility of discussion but also of 'digging' below the surface to try to reach something, ideas perhaps, not easily apparent or visible. Embedded in such a project are difficult notions, not simply defined, such as values and beliefs. Combined with this is the fact that this is about 'early years' teachers who are differently positioned and often perceived, in relation to clearly defined roles and responsibilities; whose remit inevitably spans education and care and who may appear to be less visibly accountable in relation to conventional measures of effectiveness in teaching involving physical outcomes and written performance. The way ahead, into this study, could be seen as complex, which is analogous of teaching and learning itself, as constructed in this study.

As the phase of the 'early years' of education is often seen to be at the academically lighter end of the schooling spectrum, often characterised as cutting and sticking, paint and sand (see examples, Anning 2005: 17), so too is qualitative research still often seen as not scientific and so potentially less rigorous than positivist approaches (see discussion in Holliday 2002; also Hughes and Sharrock 1997). While positivists claim the existence of a single objective reality (Pring 2004), the qualitative paradigm, in which this study rests, will recognise the interpretative nature of records of observations and the kind of social research methods used when examining people, their language and their lives (Robson 2002). It would be attractive in many ways to seek out a positivist approach to defend the phase against charges of soft subjectivity, to believe that there is a world of facts 'out there' to be discovered and publicly revealed but I believe that they are not to be found. Nor, in fact, has this ever been the case, whichever paradigm was being claimed, and indeed attempts to do so would be misguided. As Hughes and Sharrock claim: 'Facts did not just appear. They were not just lying around to be picked up by some wandering scientist; they had to be discovered, assembled and made informative' (1997: 47), with application of all of the personal states that this would require.

Understanding people, listening to children and their teachers and hearing teachers' narratives of practice, all clearly indicate the essentially human nature of this study and also therefore the complexity of a research study and findings resulting in this kind of practice. And so too, my ideas, those of the children and their teachers will naturally permeate every stage of the study including choice of observations, choice of events with children to be filmed, what is written and recorded and ultimately how it is understood and reported. My own professional heritage cannot help but be the ground on which this work sits, providing a history which itself is also socially created, both then – in my beginnings as a teacher – and now, and politically constructed. In one sense then, as researcher and inevitably interpreter, this study has been filtered through my lens, my sense of reality, my professional 'knowing'. It could be seen that this places the work outside of a post-structuralist paradigm which would give equal voice to all participants. In this kind of study inevitably the researcher's voice is paramount as the author, and the final word is always hers.

Creating a research narrative from teacher/learner narratives suggests a clear fitness for purpose in order to achieve the intentions set out previously, that is, the purpose of understanding the nature of teaching and teachers in the early years by examining their role in storying with children in play contexts. A quantitative approach would not afford the opportunities that a 'storying methodology' provides, of allowing the participants to narrativise their experiences and co-join in the research process and discussion of their practice. In this study, statistical significance is not a consideration but, instead, significance and integrity are claimed through the richness of the storying layers, through thick description and a critical, reflective narrative. The first signifiers are the teachers whose practice is being interrogated, in the company of a researcher who is having practice explained to her, even though she may already be familiar with some of the arguments. In itself this is an interesting phenomenon as the researcher appears to be seeking information as though she were a novice and, in addition, her collaborators are clearly aware of her philosophy of education. There is more to say about this in a later section.

Research principles

A key feature of this study is that it provides collaborative opportunities for 'evaluative deliberation' (Carr 2000) with the close involvement of all participants. Any study of people can take on an approach of making sense of individuals and their practice by questioning, interviewing, attempting to deconstruct their drives and intentions in a psychological sense, connected to the often cited, and perhaps overly caricatured, Piagetian notions of investigating children in laboratory conditions as if they are a 'lone scientist', constructing their own individual meanings. Or, alternatively, research can attempt to fill in the potentially blank spaces around individuals to provide a substantially richer cultural image. Super and Harkness use a useful metaphor in their anthropological research of developing an image of 'a person richly attired in ceremonial garments and surrounded by friends and kin, behaving in a way unique to that particular setting and to the larger culture which creates it' (Super and Harkness 1986: 546). This metaphor is particularly apposite in relation to early years education, if not education itself, which is traditionally heavily wrapped in layers of ritual, convention, symbols and saturated practices. Observing 'robed' professionals, examining those robes and other symbolic and ritualistic symbols, in the company of and in collaboration with these teachers will contribute to the development of a theory of practice. Continuing with the metaphor, unwrapping layers of intention, influence and beliefs of teachers will help to acknowledge and identify both the 'situational' and 'substantial' self of the teachers (Nias 1999: 20).

Studying teachers alone, then, outside of the cultural context in which they are professionally of interest, is insufficient. However, storying spaces in classrooms are of particular interest, because they are frequently if not continuously available and so easily observable. Such storying contexts (see Box 8.1) also make evident the personal investment of the child and the teacher in relation to the time given, her/his physical presence and the absorption and engagement of those participating. Further, the intentions of teachers become clearly visible in using stories and storymaking to 'socialise, acculturate and educate' (Kiesling and Bratt Paulston 2005: 13) all conventional 'saturated practices' of early years and primary classrooms.

While the intentions of teachers may become transparent to observers, it may be rather more of a challenge to identify and understand the intentions of children in storying. Although the observation and study of children at play are not the intentional focus of this work, they do have some importance if only in the reciprocal, intersubjective role they play in storying relationships. It is often claimed that children use play and therefore narratives of play or story play as self-portrait (Schieffelin and Ochs 1986). Stories and play and story play then are said to 'provide a window on the lives and identities' (Holmes 2005: 112) of those involved and can also be a way of presenting a sense of self. However, teachers are particularly influential in the early stages of children's schooling and can readily map their own intentions, and the plans of policy-makers, onto those of children. There could be opportunities therefore within storymaking to manipulate and shape children's

---

Box 8.1 Storying events

Children are serving their own intentions in play and constructing stories to narrate, to inform and to support that play.

A *teacher* (in this study, a title conferred on all adults intentionally concerned with children's learning) observes, listens and interacts with storying children in order to offer care and support to the child and/or confirm, consolidate, inform, or extend the learning opportunity. The interaction may take the form of physical presence, gesturing or oral interjections.

The *researcher* intends to observe, note, review and discuss such events with teachers.

self-seeking play. Unwrapping this particular aspect of the teacher's attire presents cultural, educational and moral implications. Indeed, Bernstein suggests that play contexts in classrooms provide opportunities for teachers to under-take 'surveillance' of children's cognitive development (1997). Bernstein's theory is that the 'spontaneity of the child is filtered through this surveillance and then implicitly shaped according to interpretation, evaluation and diagnosis' (ibid.: 60). Bernstein's notions of invisible pedagogies and his theory of teacher responses to child spontaneity in play can be associated with the ways in which teachers attempt to co-construct with children their stories in play. Further consideration also needs to be given to study of cultures of power and the use of language to symbolise that power in classroom contexts.

Discovering how much of teachers' storying activities are consciously or explicitly planned or intended has been central to this study and helps to provide an image of either intuitive, invisible or intentional practice.

Research structures

The starting point of this study was to develop an ethnographic account of such storying events in school contexts, informed also in part by biographical information of those teachers involved, thereby including elements of a life history paradigm. However, this began to appear as two separate studies, although both aspects were important in beginning to understand storying and its potential impact on children's learning. In an attempt to clarify these issues and unify the study, the research was refined to present a version of teaching realities by generating a theory in relation to storying *relationships* and thus introducing elements of grounded theory research. In effect, it then became a study with distinct but overlapping elements. The first identified and underlined the assumption that storying events are significant, the second examined the 'essence' of storying teachers and the third attempted to establish the nature of storying relationships. In order to understand all of these elements and to create a coherent picture, it has been important to interrogate the actions, interactions, processes and the people involved in storying. The study then became a hybrid of ethnography and grounded theory (Robson 2002).

If research generally involves 'a dialogue with self' (Clough 2002: 95) or 'analyses the dilemmas of self' (Robson 2002: 167), then this research exposed and examined layers of discursive opportunities, layers of narrative: child and self, child and teacher, teacher and self, teacher and researcher, researcher and self. To effect this, my research can be further described as including an *ethnography of speaking*, which Duranti describes as the study of 'language use as displayed in the daily life of particular speech communities' (Duranti 2005: 17). Such ethnographic practice can then encompass the close observa-tion of teachers 'in action' through field study and video as well as the dis-cursive opportunity offered to individual participants gathered as an intimate community to reflect upon praxis.

In this way it was possible also to construct a 'storying methodology' (Clough 2002: 4), straddling as it does the narrative form and the offer of conventional forms of data for analysis, by both researcher and readers. Clough claims that lives studied in research are often sanitised by the research process, 'steam cleaned' rather than 'stripped from the structure and protections of the traditional genre of research report [to] demonstrate the actualities of life' (ibid.: 4). Although it is seductive, Clough's research approach of fictional narrative would not be wholly sufficient for the purpose of this study as, first, it may prevent the opportunity of looking beyond the individual to the detail of broader philosophical, political and policy contexts in support of analysis and, second, the research is to be undertaken in the company of the participants rather than separate from them. The idea that post-modern research requires less of a critical perspective and review and, instead, is to be merely exemplified (Clough 2002) was simply not sufficient in my study as the core of this project has been to join with the participants in retrospectively examining their storying events. However, Clough's view that the 'task of the researcher is so to dispose words that they tell a story ... about the phenomena from which they draw their meaning' (ibid.: 10) *was* attractive in this study of people and their actions. His encouragement for some researchers to 'develop the capacity to make art' (ibid.: 9) is specifically seductive in a study that embraces storytelling and storytellers. So, by developing an ethnography of speaking where 'talk is always constitutive of some portion of reality: it either makes something already existing present to (or for) the participants or creates something anew' (Duranti 2005: 28) and presenting this in stripped bare narrative forms, it seems possible to make visible in this research the 'essence' of practitioner and practice.

Generating and collecting the data: research instruments

The collection of data occurred through the use of a small range of strategies across two stages. The data are drawn from biographical material, field notes from observations, notes from discussion groups and video material. The two-staged approach was created in order to provide time for consideration, reflection and adaptation of the material. In Stage 1, three data collection instruments are used in combination. Interview sessions have been constructed; in order to collect simple biographical material and to introduce details of the study, including the request for video material to be collected in relation to the focus. Observations were then carried out during informal sessions with the children and, following these, short debriefing conversations took place. The final session of Stage 1 was a discussion group for the purpose of sharing observation notes, film and current understandings.

Stage 2 began with a second discussion group, again sharing film and discussing issues relating to practice. The second observation included the gathering of field notes. This was followed by a lengthy conversation in which participants reviewed the session observed and summarised their practice. Between the two stages it was also important for the participants to receive a copy of transcripts and any interpretative notes, in order to gather agreement that these reflected the discussions, and to have an opportunity to edit, insert or delete, where they felt necessary. This process was repeated at the end of Stage 2.

As I discussed earlier, this project could simply have been undertaken through interviews and observations. However, there is always the persistent concern of only offering a partial view and I decided therefore to include as broad and as deep a version of intentions and events as possible.

My intention then is to incorporate the following kind of reflective view of the world of research:

> Autobiography, if there really is such a thing, is like asking a rabbit to tell us what he looks like hopping through the grasses of the field. How would he know? If we want to hear about the field, on the other hand, no one is in a better circumstance to tell us – so long as we keep in mind that we are missing all those things the rabbit was in no position to observe.
>
> (Golden 1997: v)

As I tried to understand the 'field' of storying relationships, so the ideas, interpretations and views of teachers became as valid as the ideas, interpretations and views of researchers looking on in order to collect as complete and as rich a picture of the field of study as possible.

In this study, I wished to claim the ground of 'outsider' in one sense, that is as the observer and reporter of practice and narratives of experience, but an insider in relation to the study's content and the idea of co-constructing with those observed 'versions of the truth which are woven from an amalgam of raw data, real details and symbolic equivalents' (Clough 2002: 9). And this, not for prescriptive purposes but for the more important purpose of exemplification to form a hypothesis about intuitive teachers and teaching. The idea of insider/outsider research practice also offered the opportunity, however slight, to develop the role of 'stranger' in order to further preserve a disciplined approach to the study (Holliday 2002).

There have been practical issues to consider in both the design and enactment of the study. The most demanding has been a moral concern; that is, requiring time from busy teachers to travel to come together for the purpose of discussing their practice, with no incentive other than that of tacit professional development through discursive opportunities. Teachers, in the current climate of accountability, are used to being frequently observed and teaching colleagues often generously give time to answer researchers' questions in the knowledge that this is of universal benefit. However, this project required a step further in requesting additional meeting time. The teachers were not selected for geographical convenience and they both had journeys to make as they lived and worked at opposite ends of the country. My hope has been that these colleagues would feel sufficiently motivated by the project to engage at every level, which has appeared to be the case.

A further issue here is in consideration of my position as researcher, given earlier considerations and the fact that I am known in my professional life, through teaching, research and publications, by both participants. Hence my ideological position is already very apparent and so too, therefore, the conceptual framework upon which this study is built may also have been evident to participants (Figure A1). Holliday's model makes clear the impact of acknowledged ideological positions and potential impacts on the setting and ultimately on the research.

In this model Holliday indicates points of direction, 'the ideological position' and the 'impact' on the research setting. However, in a study with elements of ethnography, impacts are invariably multi-directional and may be felt in the relationships already existing or developing, the strength of which is necessary for the free flowing of information and access. In view of the current increase in the politicisation of education, the likelihood of a

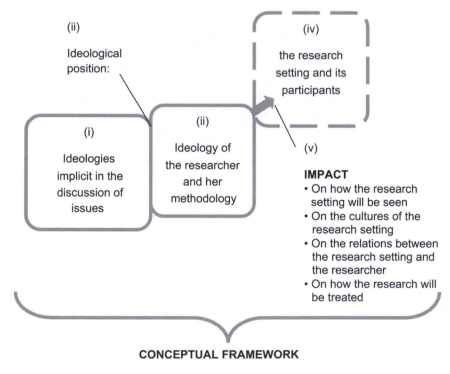

Figure A1 Conceptual framework 1

(published) school ideology being in any way similar to that of a researcher from my generation is limited and therefore an awareness of the potential for questions and challenges has been important.

From this, a new model can be constructed for the purpose of this study, giving emphasis to the potential for consensus or challenge, either of which can be productive.

Conceptual framework model

Figure A2 illustrates the potential for three ideological bases – research, school and teacher – that could exist within the research setting during the project, or indeed, shared ideologies. However, the fact that storying events exist within

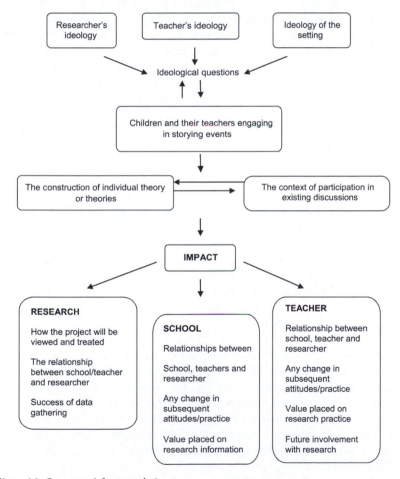

Figure A2 Conceptual framework 2

the settings suggests that this may emanate from a particular shared ideology, although ideological questions and/or challenges may also be present.

Argument for validity and reliability

In any qualitative study 'dilemmas of self' will naturally occur (Robson 2002: 167). In my study, the positioning of researcher with the experiences and assumptions carried in that role, has been seen as a positive attribute rather than a dilemma. The opportunity for open debate and honest enquiry has the potential to lead to 'reflexive self awareness' (Clough 2002: 64).

Robson uses the term 'trustworthiness' in relation to qualitative research (2002: 174), which is easy to understand as a synonym for validity in the essentially human context of this work. He suggests strategies for dealing with questions of validity and some of these can be usefully employed in this research. The first is data triangulation; that is using more than one method of data collection. In this study, a number of methods of data collection were used, for example, interview, observation and video, in order to provide a rich description of practice. In this way cross-checking of the information gathered can occur. Participants were also involved in identifying, checking, examining, discussing and reflecting upon the data to support analysis. Robson describes this as member checking and this level of rigour in cross-referencing research material by participants helps to ensure the trustworthiness of the analysis and interpretations.

There are inevitably issues inherent in any discussion of validity. If this work is 'my way of seeing that world that I both create and inhabit' (Clough 2002: 9), then it is difficult to see how that can be validated and by whom. The existence of the event and some of the elements can be verified by each teacher. However, the interpretation of such events could be individual, with overlapping spaces, areas of agreement which may emerge, while still *the truth of what is interpreted* is a dialogue with self (ibid.: 95, his italics). The 'self' in this context could be defined as that of the teachers or the researcher. The research could be described as reliable and therefore 'trustworthy' if the methods are seen to be appropriate for everybody involved, the setting and the needs of the investigation.

All of the materials gathered were shared and discussed with the participants individually and, with their permission, deconstructed, discussed and analysed in group sessions with both present. Opportunities were provided for individuals to edit transcripts and video material. As the research has been grounded in classroom acts and speech events, the detail of the interview questions has effectively emerged from observations and has been fine-tuned through the process, with the use of additional prompts where necessary.

My research has been deliberately centred upon the work of only two teachers. This research is about people; their identity, their sense of self as early years professionals, their personal and professional mentors, their family

influences and their work, from the inside out. In view of this, it felt important to me to retain the teachers' own names rather than rename them so
that, in this research story, they were truly reflected as who they are. However, the decision to do so has been their own and, while verbally they freely
gave their permission, written consent was also submitted.

Reporting on the research

Children's spontaneity and often unpredictable behaviour and playfulness,
along with the subsequent responses of their teachers, while being of central
worth to this research, also preclude the use of very structured observation
schedules in favour of the collection of descriptive narratives. The potential
richness of such descriptions will always provide ample material for consideration. However, it is the behaviour, language and human interactions of
the two teaching professionals that form the basis of this study and the
children's play and the children themselves in a sense form the backcloth – if
an engaging and delightful backcloth. Working as an intimate research
community with two reflective colleagues has helped with the interrogation
of data and to maintain clarity of focus. Inevitably, the final presentation of
the work, the final analysis of the data and the participants' comments on the
data, are the researcher's domain. That is, the final narrative layer of this
study must remain my responsibility.

Clough's (2002) notion of stripping the data bare and using the narrative
form to 'demonstrate the actualities of life' has become the most attractive
approach to constructing this research report. The transcripts, field notes and
video material were trawled through for the purpose of creating categories
and themes to support analyses and discussion. The intention has been to
classify the transcribed responses under the heading of the identified themes.
This process has been interesting. However, eventually these classification
terms and themes have been absorbed into the bigger picture of who the
teachers say they are and how they can then be described. An example of this
is that 'selfhood' and conversation relating to self-making are acknowledged
as a theme in the conversations. While this is not a separate element in the
final analysis, it is reflected in the five broad areas listed as key elements of
the teachers' knowledge, the list of their skills, the subsequent headings
under which their practice is described and finally the eight distinctive
aspects of practice. These final defining aspects of practice emerged only at
the final stages of the study, when all the material had been gathered, analysed,
themed and discussed. It then became possible to evaluate the teachers'
professional activities in this holistic way.

Although this model begins with the child, all narratives are essentially
interconnected and potentially interwoven and represent the intersubjectivity
of this kind of research into, during and in reflection upon discursive acts. At
an initial stage then, the intention was to search for themes within the

narratives, to recognise similarities between the practice observed, to collect any key vocabulary and to recognise patterns or anomalies. These activities have been of course my responsibility and themes have emerged through the process. However, it is a feature of this study that all of the above is also undertaken in the company of the two teachers so that together constructions can be made of the emerging theory/theories.

At each stage of this process, the material has required close readings and examination and continued reflection on the research questions to retain focus. However, at all stages the emphasis has remained as the construction of a research story, to illustrate the storying practices of the teachers in order to ultimately understand and define the intuitive nature of such practice. At all times the intertextual nature of these story narratives, as exemplified in the model below, has been important.

Watching children construct story play, observing, recording and discussing storying relationships (the ethnography of speaking), engaging in collaborative analysis, constructing research narratives are all interwoven threads of the same cloth. These layers or interweaving narratives are itemised in Figure A3.

In conclusion, the single most significant element of this study has been to gather narrative evidence of the lives and experiences of two teachers of young children. This required them to reveal and articulate their aims, values and beliefs in relation to teaching and learning, their constructs of children, families and childhood and to record practice that illustrated all of this. These are enormous demands to make, of anyone, at any time in their lives and it could only succeed if a trusting relationship existed between researcher and

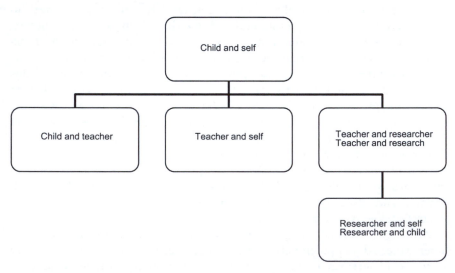

Figure A3 Interweaving narratives

those researched. The formation of a temporary and intimate group, none of whom had prior access to 'truth' was important, with this sense of equality predominating. In his comments on critical theory, Furlong acknowledges the problems involved in creating a discourse encompassing beliefs and values (2000). He claims that: 'such discourses can only happen between participants who come together as equals' and offers Habermas's conceptualisation of this as 'the ideal speech situation … although counterfactual' (ibid.: 27). This way of getting as close to what drives two teachers as possible, although providing 'a sense of equality', still retained the authority of the researcher as prompt, questioner, challenger, record keeper and reporter and so true equality could not exist. However, researching and reflecting a 'relational pedagogy' (Papatheodorou and Moyles 2008) seemed to require a relational research pedagogy and this study is as close to that as I could possibly achieve.

Bibliography

Abbott, L. (2001) 'Perceptions of play – a question of priorities?', in L. Abbott and C. Nutbrown (eds) *Experiencing Reggio Emilia: Implications for Pre-school Provision*, Buckingham: Open University Press.

Adams, S. (2005) 'Practitioners and play: reflecting in a different way', in J. Moyles (ed.) *The Excellence of Play*, 2nd edn, Maidenhead: Open University Press.

Alexander, R. (1992) *Policy and Practice in Primary Education*, London: Routledge.

——(2000) *Culture and Pedagogy*, Oxford: Blackwell.

——(2003) 'Oracy, literacy and pedagogy: international perspectives', in E. Bearne, H. Dombey and T. Grainger (eds) *Interactions in Language and Literacy in the Classroom*, Maidenhead: Open University Press.

——(ed.) (2010) *Children, their World, their Education*, London: Routledge.

Allport, G. W. (1955) *Becoming*, New Haven, CT: Yale University Press.

Anning, A. (1994) 'Play and legislated curriculum: back to basics: an alternative view', in J. Moyles (ed.) *The Excellence of Play*, Maidenhead: Open University Press.

——(2004) 'The co-construction of an early childhood curriculum', in A. Anning, J. Cullen and M. Fleer (eds) *Early Childhood Education, Society and Culture*, London: Sage.

——(2005) 'Play and legislated curriculum: back to basics: an alternative view', in J. Moyles (ed.) *The Excellence of Play*, 2nd edn, Maidenhead: Open University Press.

Anning, A., Cullen, J. and Fleer, M. (2004) *Early Childhood Education, Society and Culture*, London: Sage.

Apple, M. W. (2004) 'Cultural politics and the text', in S. J. Ball (ed.) *The RoutledgeFalmer Reader in Sociology of Education*, London: RoutledgeFalmer.

Atkinson, T. and Claxton, G. (2000) *The Intuitive Practitioner on the Value of Not Always Knowing What One Is Doing*, Buckingham: Open University Press.

Bakhtin, M. M. (1981) *The Dialogic Imagination*, Austin, TX: University of Texas Press.

——(1986) *Speech Genres and Other Late Essays*, trans. V. McGee, ed. C. Emerson and M. Holquist, Austin, TX: University of Texas Press.

Ball, S. J. (ed.) (2004) *The RoutledgeFalmer Reader in Sociology of Education*, London: RoutledgeFalmer.

——(2005) 'The "childcare champion"? New Labour, social justice and the childcare market', *British Educational Research Journal*, 31(5): 557–70.

——(2008) *The Education Debate*, Bristol: The Policy Press.

Balls, E. (2007) 'The Every Child Matters Department', keynote speech at event hosted by the National Children's Bureau, the Business Design Centre, Islington, July.

Barrs, M. (1988) 'Maps of play' in M. Meek and C. Mills (eds) *Language and Literacy in the Primary School*, Lewes: Falmer Press.

BBC (2003) 'Woman's Hour, children and nursery rhymes', 7 July 2003. Available at: www. bbc.co.uk.

——(2008) 'Newsround: Mosquito deters nuisance youths', 12 February 2008. Available at: www.bbc.co.uk.

Bearne, E. (2002) *Making Progress in Writing*, London: RoutledgeFalmer.

——(2003) 'Rethinking literacy: communication, representation and text', *Reading Literacy and Language*, 37(3): 98–103.

Bennett, J. (2005) 'Curriculum issues in national policy making', *European Early Childhood Research Journal*, 13(2): 5–23.

Bennett, J. and Organisation for Economic Cooperation and Development (2006) *Starting Strong 11, Early Childhood Education and Care*, Paris: OECD.

Bennett, N. (1976) *Teaching Styles and Pupil Progress*, London: Open Books Publishing Limited.

BERA SIG (British Educational Research Association Early Years Special Interest Group) (2003) *Review of Early Years Research: Pedagogy, Curriculum and Adult Roles*, Southwell: British Educational Research Association.

Bernstein, B. (1977) *Class, Codes and Control: Toward a Theory of Educational Transmission*, 2nd edn, London: Routledge & Kegan Paul.

——(1997) 'Class and pedagogies: visible and invisible', in A.H. Halsley, H. Lauder, P. Brown and A. S. Wells (eds) *Education, Culture, Economy, Society*, Oxford: Oxford University Press.

Bettelheim, B. (1978) *The Uses of Enchantment: The Meaning and Importance of Fairy Tales*, London: Penguin.

——(1982) *On Learning to Read: The Child's Fascination with Meaning*, London: Thames and Hudson.

Blakemore, S. J. and Frith, U. (2005) *The Learning Brain: Lessons for Education*, Oxford: Blackwell.

Brice Heath, S. (1983) *Ways with Words*, Cambridge: Cambridge University Press.

Britton, J. (1970) *Language and Learning: The Importance of Speech in Children's Development*, London: Penguin.

Bronfenbrenner, U. (ed.) (1972) *Influences on Human Development*, Hinsdale, IL: The Dryden Press Inc.

——(1979) *The Ecology of Human Development*, Cambridge, MA: Harvard University Press.

Brown, S. (2003) 'Celebrating childhood', keynote address to the 13th Annual Conference of the European Early Childhood Education Research Association, Quality in Early Education: Possible Childhoods – Relationships and Choices, University of Strathclyde, Glasgow.

Bruce, T. (1987) *Early Childhood Education*, Sevenoaks: Hodder and Stoughton.

——(1994) 'Play, the universe and everything!', in J. Moyles (ed.) *The Excellence of Play*, Maidenhead: Open University Press.

——(2005) 'Play, the universe and everything!', in J. Moyles (ed.) *The Excellence of Play*, 2nd edn, Maidenhead: Open University Press.

Bruner, J. (1964) 'The course of cognitive growth', *American Psychologist*, 19: 1–15.

——(1986) *Actual Minds, Possible Worlds*, Cambridge, MA: Harvard University Press.

——(2000) 'Foreword', in J. DeLoache and A. Gottlieb (eds) *A World of Babies*, Cambridge: Cambridge University Press.

——(2002) *Making Stories: Law, Literature, Life*, Cambridge, MA: Harvard University Press.

Bruner, J. and Haste, H. (eds) (1987) *Making Sense: The Child's Construction of the World*, London: Methuen & Co Ltd.

Bryan, H. (2004) 'Constructs of teacher professionalism within a changing literacy landscape', *Literacy*, 38(3): 141–8.

Campbell, E. (2003) *The Ethical Teacher*, Buckingham: Open University Press.

Carr, D. (2000) *Professionalism and Ethics in Teaching*, London: RoutledgeFalmer.

Carreira da Silva, F. (2007) *G. H. Mead: A Critical Introduction*, Cambridge: Polity Press.

Carter, R. (2004) *Language and Creativity: The Art of Common Talk*, London: Routledge.

Central Advisory Council for Education (1967) *Children and their Primary Schools* (the Plowden Report), London: HMSO.

Children's Workforce Development Council (2008) *Early Years Home Page*. Available at: www.cwdcouncil.org.uk/early-years.

Claxton, G. (2000) 'The anatomy of intuition', in T. Atkinson and G. Claxton (eds) *The Intuitive Practitioner*, Buckingham: Open University Press.

Clough, P. (2002) *Narratives and Fictions in Educational Research*, Buckingham: Open University Press.

Cole, M. (1998) 'Culture in development', in M. Woodhead, D. Faulkner and K. Littleton *Cultural Worlds of Early Childhood*, London: Routledge and the Open University Press.

Dahlberg, G. (2000) 'Everything is a beginning and everything is dangerous: some reflections on the Reggio Emilia experience', in H. Penn (ed.) *Early Childhood Services: Theory, Policy and Practice*, Buckingham: Open University Press.

Dahlberg, G. and Moss, P. (2005) *Ethics and Politics in Early Childhood Education*, London: RoutledgeFalmer.

Dahlberg, G., Moss, P. and Pence, A. (1999) *Beyond Quality in Early Childhood Education and Care: Postmodern Perspectives*, London: RoutledgeFalmer.

Daniels, H. (1999) *Teaching Young Children*, London: Paul Chapman.

——(2007) 'Pedagogy', in H. Daniels, M. Cole and J.V. Wertsch (eds) *The Cambridge Companion to Vygotsky*, New York: Cambridge University Press.

David, T. (2007) 'Birth to Three: the need for a loving and educated workforce', in J. Moyles (ed.) *Early Years Foundations: Meeting the Challenge*, Maidenhead: Open University Press.

David, T., Goouch, K., Powell, S. and Abbott, L. (2003) *Birth to Three Matters: A Review of the Literature*, Nottingham: DfES Publications.

David, T., Raban, B., Ure, C., Goouch, K., Jago, M., Barriere, I., and Lambirth, A. (2000) *Making Sense of Early Literacy: A Practitioner's Perspective*, Stoke on Trent: Trentham.

DeLoache, J. and Gottlieb, A. (2000) *A World of Babies*, Cambridge: Cambridge University Press.

Department for Education and Science (1990) *Starting with Quality: Report of the Committee of Enquiry into the Quality of Education and Experience Offered to Three and Four Year Olds*, Rumbold Report, London: HMSO.

Department for Children, Schools and Families (2007) *The Early Years Foundation Stage*, London: DCSF.

Department for Education and Skills (2004) *Every Child Matters: Change for Children*, London: DfES/HM Government.

——(2005) *Higher Standards, Better Schools for All*, Nottingham: DfES.

——(2006a) *Independent Review of the Teaching of Early Reading* (The Rose Review), London: DfES.

——(2006b) *The Primary National Strategy*, Nottingham: DfES.

Department for Education and Skills/Surestart (2003) *Birth to Three Matters: A Framework to Support Children in Their Earliest Years*, London: DfES Publications.

Desforges, C. (2000) *Familiar Challenges and New Approaches: Necessary Advances in Theory and Methods in Research on Teaching and Learning*, Southwell: BERA.

Drummond, M. J. (2001) 'Foreword', in S. Jenkinson, *The Genius of Play: Celebrating the Spirit of Childhood*, Stroud: Hawthorn Press.

Duffy, B. (2010) 'The Early Years curriculum', in G. Pugh and B. Duffy (eds) *Contemporary Issues in the Early Years*, London: Sage.

Dunn, J. (1998) 'Young children's understanding of other people: evidence from observations within the family', in M. Woodhead (ed.) *Cultural Worlds of Early Childhood*, London: Routledge/Open University.

——(2004) *Children's Friendships: The Beginnings of Intimacy*, Oxford: Blackwell.

Duranti, A. (2005) 'Ethnography of speaking: toward a linguistic of the praxis', in S. F. Kiesling and C. B. Paulston (eds) *Intercultural Discourse and Communication: The Essential Readings*, Oxford: Blackwell.

Durkheim, E. (1956) *Education and Society*, New York: The Free Press.

Egan, K. (2003) 'The cognitive tools of children's imagination', in B. Van Oers (ed.) *Narratives of Childhood: Theoretical and Practical Explorations for the Innovation of Early Childhood Education*, Amsterdam: VU University Press.

Ellis, S. (2007) 'Policy and research: lessons from the Clackmannanshire Synthetic Phonics Initiative' in *Journal of Early Childhood Literacy*, 7(3): 281–299.

Fox, C. (1988) 'Poppies will make them grant', in M. Meek and C. Mills (eds) *Language and Literacy in the Primary School*, Lewes: Falmer.

Frayne, M. (2006) *The Human Touch*, London: Faber and Faber.

Freire, P. (1976) *Education, the Practice of Freedom*, London: Writers and Readers Publishing Cooperative.

Freire, P. and Macedo, D. (1987) *Literacy: Reading the Word and the World*, London: Routledge.

Furlong, J. (2000) 'Intuition and the crisis in teacher professionalism', in T. Atkinson and G. Claxton (eds) *The Intuitive Practitioner*, Buckingham: Open University Press.

Gardner, H. (2004) 'The hundred languages of successful educational reform', *Children in Europe*, 6: 16–17.

Geekie, P., Cambourne, B. and Fitzsimmons, P. (1999) *Understanding Literacy Development*, Stoke on Trent: Trentham.

Gerhardt, S. (2004) *Why Love Matters: How Affection Shapes a Baby's Brain*, London: Routledge.

Gibson, H. and Patrick, H. (2008) 'Putting words in their mouths: the role of teaching assistants and the spectre of scripted pedagogy', *Journal of Early Childhood Literacy*, 8(1): 25–41.

Giroux, H. A. (1987) 'Introduction: literacy and the pedagogy of political empowerment', in P. Freire and D. Macedo, *Literacy: Reading the Word and the World*, London: Routledge.

Golden, A. (2005) *Memoirs of a Geisha*, London: Vintage.

Goodley, D., Lawthorm, R. and Clough, P. (2004) *Researching Life Stories, Method, Theory and Analysis in a Biographical Age*, London: RoutledgeFalmer.

Gopnik, A. (2009) *The Philosophical Baby*, London: The Bodley Head.

Gopnik, A., Meltzoff, A. and Kuhl, P. (1999) *How Babies Think*, London: Weidenfeld and Nicolson.

Grainger, T. (1997) 'Poetry from the nursery and the playground: making time for rhythms and rhymes', *Language and Learning*, 7: 12–16.

Grainger, T. and Goouch, K. (1999) 'Young children and playful language', in T. David (ed.) *Teaching Young Children*, London: Paul Chapman.

Grainger, T., Goouch, K. and Lambirth, A (2005) *Creativity and Writing: Developing Voice and Verve in the Classroom*, London: Routledge.

Greenfield, S. (2000) *The Private Life of the Brain*, London: Penguin.

Grenfell, M. and James, D. (1998) *Bourdieu and Education*, London: Falmer.

Hall, K. (2004) *Literacy and Schooling: Towards Renewal in Primary Education Policy*, Hampshire: Ashgate.

——(2007) 'A Wengerian perspective on early literacy policy in England', in K. Goouch and A. Lambirth (eds) *Understanding Phonics and the Teaching of Reading*, Maidenhead: Open University Press.

Hall, N. (1987) *The Emergence of Literacy*, Sevenoaks: Hodder and Stoughton.

——(1999) 'Young children, play and literacy: engagement in realistic uses of literacy', in J. Marsh and E. Hallet (eds) *Desirable Literacies: Approaches to Language and Literacy in the Early Years*, London: Paul Chapman.

Halpin, D and Troyna, B. (eds) (1994) *Researching Education Policy: Ethical and Methodological Issues*, London: Falmer.

Hardy, B. (1977) 'Narrative as a primary act of mind', in M. Meek, A. Warlow and G. Barton (eds) *The Cool Web*, London: The Bodley Head.

Hartley, D. (1993) *Understanding the Nursery School*, London: Cassell.

——(2006) 'The instrumentalization of the expressive in education', in A. Moore (ed.) *Schooling, Society and Curriculum*, London: Routledge.

Heaney, S. (2006) *Death of a Naturalist*, London: Faber and Faber.

Holliday, A. (2002) *Doing and Writing Qualitative Research*, London: Sage.

——(2008) 'Submission, emergence and personal knowledge: new takes and principles for validity in decentred qualitative research', unpublished article.

Holquist, M. (1981) 'Introduction', in M.M. Bakhtin, *The Dialogic Imagination*, ed M. Holquist, trans. C. Emerson and M. Holquist, Austin, TX: University of Texas Press.

Hughes, J. and Sharrock, W. (1997) *The Philosophy of Social Research*, 3rd edn, Harlow: Longman.

Hynds, G. (2007) 'Putting a spin on reading: the language of the Rose Review', *Journal of Early Childhood Literacy*, 7(3): 267–81.

Immordino-Yang, M. H. and Damasio, A. (2007) 'We feel, therefore we learn: the relevance of affective and social neuroscience to education', *Mind, Brain and Education*, 1(1): 3–10.

Jenkinson, S. (2001) *The Genius of Play: Celebrating the Spirit of Childhood*, Stroud: Hawthorn Press.

Karmiloff, K. and Karmiloff-Smith, A. (2001) *Pathways to Language: From Fetus to Adolescent*, Cambridge, MA: Harvard University Press.

Katz, L. (2007) 'Mothering and teaching: some significant distinctions', presentation to OMEP (UK), Institute of Education, London.

Kelchterman, G. (1993) 'Teachers and their career story', in C. Day, J. Calderhead and P. Denicolo (eds) *Research on Teacher Thinking: Understanding Professional Development*, London: Falmer.

Kenner, C. (2004) *Becoming Biliterate: Young Children Learning Different Writing Systems*, Stoke-on-Trent: Trentham.

Kiesling, S. F. and Bratt Paulston, C. (2005) *Intercultural Discourse and Communication*, Oxford: Blackwell.

Kress, G. (1997) *Before Writing: Rethinking the Paths to Literacy*, London: Routledge.

——(2000) *Early Spelling: Between Convention and Creativity*, London: Routledge.

Lacey, C. (1977) 'The socialisation of teachers', cited in S. Ball (ed.) *The RoutledgeFalmer Reader in Sociology of Education*, London: RoutledgeFalmer.

Lambirth, A. (2003) '"They get enough of that at home": understanding aversion to popular culture in schools', *Reading, Literacy and Language*, 37(1): 9–13.

Lambirth, A. and Goouch, K. (2006) 'Golden times of writing: the creative compliance of writing journals', *Literacy, Reading and Language*, 40(3): 146–52.

Lawrence, D. H. (1972) 'Thought', in *Selected Poems*, Harmondsworth: Penguin.

Lubeck, S. (1986) *Sandbox Society*. London: Falmer Press.

McGregor, J. (2002) *If Nobody Speaks of Remarkable Things …* , London: Bloomsbury.

——(2004) 'Space, power and the classroom', *Forum*, 46(1): 13–18.

McLean, S. V. (1991) *The Human Encounter: Teachers and Children Living Together in Preschools*, London: Falmer Press.

Malaguzzi, L. (2004) 'Walking on threads of silk', *Children in Europe*, 6: 10–15.

Marsh, J, (2005) *Popular Culture, New Media and Digital Literacy in Early Childhood*, London: RoutledgeFalmer.

Marsh, J. and Millard, E. (2000) *Literacy and Popular Culture*, London: Paul Chapman.

Matthews, J. (1999) *The Art of Childhood and Adolescence*, London: Falmer.

May, H. (2002) 'Early childhood care and education in Aotearoa – New Zealand: an overview of history, policy and curriculum', *McGill Journal of Education*, 37(1): 19–36.

Medwell, J., Wray, D., Poulson, L. and Fox, R. (1997) *Effective Teachers of Literacy*, Exeter: University of Exeter Press.

Meek, M. (1985) 'Play and paradoxes: some considerations of imagination and language', in G. Wells and J. Nicholls (eds) *Language and Learning: An International Perspective*, London: Falmer.

Meltzoff, A. (2002) 'Imitation as a mechanism of social cognition: origins of empathy, theory of mind, and the representation of action', in U. Goswami (ed.) *Childhood Cognitive Development*, Oxford: Blackwell.

Menter, I., Muschamp, Y., Nicholls, P., Ozga, J., and Pollard, A. (1997) *Work and Identity in the Primary School: A Post-Fordist Analysis*, Buckingham: Open University Press.

Mercer, N. (2000) *Words and Minds: How We Use Language to Think Together*, London: Routledge.

Moss, P. and Petrie, P. (2002) *From Children's Services to Children's Spaces*, London: RoutledgeFalmer.

Moyles, J. (1989) *Just Playing? The Role and Status of Play in Early Childhood Education*, Buckingham: Open University Press.

——(ed.) (2005a) *The Excellence of Play*, 2nd edn, Maidenhead: Open University Press.

——(2005b) *Early Years Foundations: Meeting the Challenge*, Maidenhead: Open University Press.

Newson, J. and Newson, E. (1979) *Toys and Playthings*, Harmondsworth: Penguin.

Nias, J. (1989) *Primary Teachers Talking: A Study of Teaching as Work*, London: Routledge.

——(2006) 'Transcribing interviews: some heretical thoughts in BERA' *Research Intelligence*, 97: 12–17.

Noddings, N. (1992) *The Challenge to Care in Schools: An Alternative Approach to Education*, New York: Teachers College Press.

Nutbrown, C., Clough, P and Selbie, P. (2008) *Early Childhood Education: History, Philosophy and Experience*, London: Sage.

Nutbrown, C. and Page, J. (2008) *Working with Babies and Children from Birth to Three*, London: Sage.

OECD (Organisation for Economic Co-Operation and Development) (2006) *Starting Strong 11, Early Childhood Education and Care*, Paris: OECD Publishing.

Olssen, M., Codd, J. and O'Neill, A. M. (2004) *Education Policy, Globalisation, Citizenship and Democracy*, London: Sage.

Open Eye Campaign (2007) Available at: www.guardian.co.uk.

Owen, S. and Haynes, G. (2010) 'Training and workforce issues in the early years', in G. Pugh and B. Duffy (eds) *Contemporary Issues in the Early Years*, London: Sage.

Pahl, K. (1999) *Transformations: Meaning Making in Nursery Education*, Stoke-on-Trent: Trentham.

Papatheodorou, T. and Moyles, J. (2008) *Learning Together in the Early Years: Relational Pedagogy*, London: RoutledgeFalmer.

Pence, A. and Ball, J. (2000) 'Two sides of an eagle's feather: University of Victoria partnerships with Canada First Nations Communities', in H. Penn (ed.) *Early Childhood Services: Theory, Policy and Practice*, Buckingham: Open University Press.

Peters, R. S. (1966) *Ethics and Education*, London: George Allen & Unwin Ltd.

Piaget, J. (1959) *The Language and Thought of the Child*, London: Routledge and Kegan Paul Ltd.

Pollard, A. (2004) 'Towards a sociology of learning in primary schools', in S. J. Ball, *The RoutledgeFalmer Reader in Sociology of Education*, London: RoutledgeFalmer.

Pring, R. (2004) *Philosophy of Education*, London: Continuum.

Pugh, G. (2010) 'The policy agenda for early childhood services', in G. Pugh and B. Duffy (eds) *Contemporary Issues in the Early Years*, London: Sage.

Pugh, G. and Duffy, B. (eds) (2010) *Contemporary Issues in the Early Years*, 5th edn, London: Sage.

QCA (2000) *Curriculum Guidance for the Foundation Stage*, London: QCA/DfEE.

Rinaldi, C. (2005) 'Documentation and assessment: what is the relationship?' in A. Clark, A. T. Kjorholt and P. Moss (eds) *Beyond Listening: Children's Perspectives on Early Childhood Services*, Bristol: The Policy Press.

Robson, C. (2002) *Real World Research*, 2nd edn, Oxford: Blackwell.

Rogoff, B. (1990) *Apprenticeship in Thinking: Cognitive Development in Social Context*, Oxford: Oxford University Press.

Rogoff, B., Mosier, C., Mistry, J. and Goncu, P. (1998) 'A toddlers' guided participation with their caregivers in cultural activity', in M. Woodhead, D. Faulkner and K. Littleton, London: Routledge.

Rosen, H. (1988) *Stories and Meanings*, NATE Papers in Education, London: National Association of Teachers in English.

Sachs, J. (2003) 'Teacher Activism: Mobilising the Profession', Plenary address presented to the British Educational Research Association Conference, Nottingham.

Sammons, P., Elliot, K., Sylva, K., Melhuish, E., Siraj-Blatchford, I. and Taggart, T. (2004) 'The impact of pre-school on young children's cognitive attainments at entry to Reception', *British Educational Research Journal*, 30(5): 691–712.

Schieffelin, B. B. and Ochs, E. (1986) *Language Socialisation across Cultures*, Cambridge: Cambridge University Press.

Shaffer, P. (1973) *Equus*, London: Andre Deutsch.

Shotter, J. (1993) *Cultural Politics of Everyday Life: Social Constructionism, Rhetoric and Knowing of the Third Kind*, Buckingham: Open University Press.

Siraj-Blatchford, I. (2004) 'Quality teaching in the early years', in A. Anning, J. Cullen, and M. Fleer, *Early Childhood Education, Society and Culture*, London: Sage.

Siraj-Blatchford, I. and Sylva, K. (2004) 'Researching pedagogy in English pre-schools', *British Educational Research Journal*, 30(5): 713–30.

Smidt, S. (2003) 'Six fingers with feeling: play, literacy and politics', in E. Bearne, H. Dombey and T. Grainger (eds) *Interactions in Language and Literacy in the Classroom*, Maidenhead: Open University Press.

Stannard, J. (1999) 'The National Literacy Strategy', keynote speech at United Kingdom Reading Association National Conference, March, Cambridge.

Steedman, C. (1982) *The Tidy House*, London: Virago.

Super, C. M. and Harkness, S. (1998) 'The development of affect in infancy and early childhood', in M. Woodhead, D. Faulkner and K. Littlejohn (eds) *Cultural Worlds of Early Childhood*, London: Routledge and The Open University.

Sutton-Smith, B. (1997) *The Ambiguity of Play*, Cambridge, MA: Harvard University Press.

Sylva, K., Melhuish, E., Sammons, P., Siraj-Blatchford, I. and Taggart, B. (2004) *Effective Provision of Pre-School Education* (EPPE) *Project*, Final Report, London: DfES, Surestart.

Tizard, B. and Hughes, M. (1984) *Young Children Learning*, London: Fontana.

Trevarthan, C. (1998) 'The child's need to learn a culture', in M. Woodhead, D. Faulkner and K. Littlejohn (eds) *Cultural Worlds of Early Childhood*, London: Routledge and Open University.

Vološinov, V. N. (1973) *Marxism and the Philosophy of Language*, Cambridge, MA: Harvard University Press.

Vygotsky, L.(1978) *Mind in Society: The Development of Higher Psychological Processes*, Cambridge, MA: Harvard University Press.

——(1986) *Thought and Language*, Cambridge, MA: MIT Press.

Wells, G. (1986) *The Meaning Makers: Children Learning Language and Using Language to Learn*, Sevenoaks: Hodder and Stoughton.

Wenger, E. (1998) *Communities of Practice: Learning, Meaning and Identity*, Cambridge: Cambridge University Press.

Wertsch, J. V. (1991) *Voices of the Mind: A Sociocultural Approach to Mediated Action*, Cambridge, MA: Harvard University Press.

——(2007) 'Vygotsky on human nature and human development', keynote address, 17th EECERA Conference, Exploring Vygotsky's Ideas: Crossing Borders, Prague.

Whitehead, M. (1997) *Language and Literacy in the Early Years*, 2nd edn, London: Sage.

——(1999a) *Supporting Language and Literacy Development in the Early Years*, Buckingham: Open University Press.

——(1999b) 'A literacy hour in the nursery? The big question mark', *Early Years*, 19(2): 38–62.

——(2004) *Language and Literacy in the Early Years*, 3rd edn, London: Sage.

Whittey, G. (1997) 'Marketization, the state and the re-formation of the teaching profession', in A. H. Halsey, H. Lauder, P. Brown and A.S. Wells (eds) *Education, Culture, Economy, Society*, Oxford: Oxford University Press.

Wood, D. (1988) *How Children Think and Learn*, Oxford: Blackwell.

Woodhead, M., Faulkner, D. and Littlejohn, K. (eds) (1998) *Cultural Worlds of Early Childhood*, London: Routledge and Open University.

Woods, P. and Jeffrey, B. (2004) 'The reconstruction of primary teachers' identities', in S. J. Ball (ed.) *The RoutledgeFalmer Reader in Sociology of Education*, London: RoutlledgeFalmer.

Yeats, W. B. (1994) *The Collected Poems of W. B. Yeats*, Ware: Wordsworth Poetry Library.

Young, M. F. D (2006) 'Education, knowledge and the role of the state: the "nationalization" of educational knowledge?', in A. Moore (ed.) *Schooling, Society and Curriculum*, London: Routledge.

Index

accountability 80, 131; audit accountability 47, 49; discourse 2; education 61; learning 85–86, 92, 109, 112–13; play 16, 49, 85, 129, 130; playful pedagogies 16, 49; policy 47; practice 19; schools in England 25; teachers 47, 138, 143; teachers of the study 80, 81, 101–2; *see also* policy
acts, agreements, laws: Childcare Act (2006) 6; Children Act (1989) 4; Education Act (1992) 4; Education Act (1996) 4; Education Reform Act (1988) 4
adult 8; addressivity 78, 80, 82, 107, 120; adults/children engagement 12, 28, 32, 67, 71, 82, 107, 140 (complexity 73); adult's role in children's dialogue 54, 55, 118; adult's role in children learning 56, 59; as knowledgeable 'insider' 58; education 43; guided participation 56, 58; intersubjectivity 48, 58, 63–64, 125, 147; mutuality 44, 58, 80, 82, 125; narrative co-constructions, formal adult-led contexts 28; play, pretend play 40, 58, 59; power 19; practice planning 85–87; 'scaffolding' 32, 56–57, 131; talk: adult's role 54, 55–57, 58, 59; talking to, talking with 56–59; *see also* play, adult's role; teacher; teachers of the study; teachers of the study, children
affective education 24, 26, 27; affective engagement 21–22, 27, 28; affective educational practices and the use of story 21–22; affective teaching and learning 21, 22, 27, 73; cognitive development/emotion relationship 22, 30; professional judgement 67, 72–73
assessment 5, 18, 90, 130; curriculum 42; EPPE started Baseline Assessment 4; Standard Attainment Tests (SATs) 7, 109

Bakhtin, Mikhail Mikhailovich: addressivity 78; complexity of speech events 57; multivoicing 121; speech genres 16; 'voice' 121; 'Who is doing the talking?' 16, 59, 80–81, 121, 122; word 57, 81, 119–20, 122, 132
Bernstein, Basil: invisible pedagogy 31, 49, 80, 114, 141; play and surveillance 21, 141; *see also* pedagogy
Birth to Three Matters: A Review of Literature 1
Bourdieu, Pierre 45, 51

child: as the centre of all services 9, 61; as expert 56, 76; adults/children engagement 12, 28, 32, 67, 71, 82, 107, 140 (complexity 73); child-centred pedagogy 81; child-led conversation/play 53, 74, 77, 88, 91–92, 97, 108, 121, 122, 130; conversational opportunities 27; human relationships in children's lives/learning 1–2, 27, 30 (tenacity in pursuing social contact 46); intentions 16, 20, 42, 44, 48, 53, 82, 103, 107, 111, 123 (at play 16, 32, 78, 101, 108, 122, 129, 132, 140; respect of intentionality 128–29); interests 20, 61, 86, 88, 90, 107, 108, 120; intersubjectivity 45, 48, 82, 140, 147; learning 17, 27, 45, 123 (child as agent of their own learning 47, 50, 109, 115, 118; teachers as 'reflective agents' in children's learning 47); 'Nordic curricular tradition' 7, 8, 12; primary stakeholder in education debates 50; reflection and metacognion 123, 127, 130; respect for children 50, 51, 71, 77, 107, 108, 113, 116; roles 45–46; 'schoolification', school curricular